GETTING THE BEST FROM

EXPOSED GARDENS

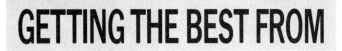

GETTING THE BEST FROM

EXPOSED
GARDENS

NIGEL COLBORN

SERIES EDITOR
ALAN TOOGOOD

WARD LOCK LIMITED · LONDON

First published in Great Britain in 1989
by Ward Lock Limited, 8 Clifford Street,
London W1X 1RB, an Egmont Company.

Designed by David Robinson

Typeset by Jamesway Graphics, Hanson Close,
Middleton, Manchester M24 2HD

Printed and bound by Rotolito, Milan, Italy

British Library Cataloguing in Publication Data

Colborn, Nigel
　Getting the best from gardening on exposed
　sites.
　1. Gardening
　I. Title
　635.9'55

　ISBN 0-7063-6760-X

Cover: *If an exposed garden is well provided with wind protection a surprisingly wide range of plants can be grown, including rhododendrons, many of which are not very tolerant of windy conditions. Dense planting, as shown here at Marwood Hill, Barnstaple, Devon, creates additional shelter.*

Previous page: Acer pseudoplatanus *'Brilliantissimum'. A neat growing tree with shrimp-pink spring foliage turning gold with age. Weather-proof but not fast growing.*

CONTENTS

INTRODUCTION

When we moved into our present home, some twelve years ago, a neighbour asked me what my interests were. 'Gardening,' I replied. She laughed. 'You can't make a garden here,' she said, 'it's far too windy and cold. That's why the locals don't bother.' But make a garden we did, and now that our first plantings of trees and hedges have grown up and filled out, visitors who do not know the area often say, 'aren't you lucky to be so sheltered here.'

Getting the Best From Exposed Gardens shows how even the bleakest locations can, with careful planning and planting, be transformed into delightful and pleasing gardens. No site, however well favoured or with whatever local climate, is perfect and, indeed, most are far from ideal.

Getting to know the prevailing conditions is the gardener's first task. Wind directions, speeds, winter temperatures, soils and local topography must all be taken into careful consideration. Once the unique advantages of the site have been identified, and the worst is known about it, work can begin to build on the 'plus' points and to eliminate as many of the drawbacks as possible. Typical problem gardens are described here and solutions to a whole range of difficulties offered.

Having discussed the planning stage in Chapters 1–3, I then go on to look in detail at the planting and each chapter recommends a collection of plants for specific uses. Starting with the backbone of trees and shrubs and going down through herbaceous perennials to small ground-huggers and crevice-fillers, plants are suggested for every part of the garden. Only the toughest and easiest species are listed and there are special sections on roses and conifers. An entire chapter is also included on 'vertical' gardening, which encompasses growing climbing and wall plants.

There is also a chapter on growing fruit and vegetables and a closing section designed not only to provide guidance for overall maintenance but also indicating how a garden can be made to provide maximum enjoyment and satisfaction.

Hollies make good windbreaks and many, like Ilex × altaclarensis *'Golden King' have decorative foliage and good berries.*

GETTING TO KNOW YOUR GARDEN

Exposed garden? No problem! When it comes to choosing your garden location, there is no such thing as an ideal site. Every place, even the most tranquil vale on the most fertile soil in the most favoured climate, will have at least one drawback. The average garden is normally far from ideal, but wherever you live, whatever soil you encounter and however cruelly your winter winds blow, there are dozens of ways in which you can minimize the bad effects. Furthermore, every garden, however unfortunate its position, will have several distinct advantages. The job of a crafty garden designer is to organize the planting and layout so that these advantages are maximized to the full, and so that the worst of the problems are either eliminated altogether or reduced to insignificance.

Whatever they are, most garden sites, particularly new ones, are often exposed. Successful gardening depends on plenty of shelter for plants, but a large number of people like to live in exposed houses, which are blessed with panoramic views. New houses are often built on hillsides or near the coast and may even be sold at a premium because of such views. However, good views normally mean exposure to winds, so for gardeners, there is a clash of interests here. Planting trees for shelter is perfectly feasible but needs to be done tactfully so that the best vistas are retained. The object of this book is to help you to take advantage of the good points of your site and to eliminate as many negative aspects as possible.

THE EXPOSED GARDEN

What is wrong with having an exposed garden? Nothing at all. Climate and soil type are aspects over which you have no control. You can im-

> *NOTE*: Plants mentioned in the first three chapters will be described in the plant directory chapters in detail.

prove poor soils to a certain extent, but nothing will convert sandy loam to chalky clay. As far as weather is concerned, even prolonged praying will fail to divert a blizzard heading in your direction, but with time and careful planning, you *can* turn an exposed garden into a sheltered one, so that when that blizzard arrives its effect is reduced. Let us first look at just what makes a garden exposed.

Wind

Wind is one of the most tiresome garden problems. It attacks plants in different ways at different times. In winter, when everything is dormant, the wind will not affect plant growth but can still inflict plenty of physical damage. Some of this can be very obvious: branches blowing off, trees being felled, climbing plants ripped off walls and so on. There is also the more subtle, insidious destruction that may not come to light until growth begins during spring. Shrubs, particularly newly planted specimens, can rock to and fro until their roots are greatly loosened. In some soils, this rocking action causes a funnel-shaped hole to develop round the base of the main stems where they disappear into the ground. Later, if this fills with water, the stem is likely to rot and the shrub or tree is lost. If that collar of water freezes a shrub's demise is even more certain.

In excessively cold areas, a frosty wind spells disaster. Everyone knows that a stiff breeze on a day where the temperature is –2°C (28°F) feels much colder than a still morning with temperatures at –8°C (18°F). Soil which is exposed to a freezing wind is penetrated to a greater depth than with a sharp overnight frost in calm weather. Woody plants, particularly evergreens, can be damaged by this 'chill factor' which may cause browning and disfiguring, even among hardy plants. Woody climbers such as honeysuckles and some of the clematis hybrids can be perfectly hardy in most gardens, but may well suffer when exposed to sustained, freezing winds. Evidence of this comes to light when spring begins and the plants in sheltered gardens produce shoots from the old wood, whereas climbers in the exposed garden have to begin again from below the ground.

In spring, wind brings a whole new set of problems. Before the plants have emerged or come into leaf, most spring gardens have considerable areas of bare soil. This can dry out excessively and where rainfall is low the soil moisture may not be replaced for some time. Spring winds can be bitterly cold and will scorch and stunt tender young growth. Tiny seedlings—normally in abundance in a good garden in early spring—can be destroyed by dehydration in a cutting spring breeze. Newly emerged buds and branches grow at a far slower rate in windy conditions and the stems are shorter and harder. In nature, this is apparent when you look at a tree which stands in an exposed site. In middle-aged specimens, the windward side is rounded and flattened towards the top because of the shortening of each branch and twig, while the leeward side looks nearly normal. As the tree ages, this lop-sided appearance gets worse until most branches of any length are pointing away from the wind and the tree becomes flat topped and completely asymmetrical. When house-hunting in an area strange to you, trees like this in the vicinity will tell you a great deal about the strength of the local winds. You may be viewing on one of the few calm days of the year!

During summer, the damage from wind is mostly

Mountain ashes make fine trees, even in cold gardens. The berries of Sorbus *'Joseph Rock' become orange with age, harmonizing with the bronze autumn foliage.*

mechanical. Roses, for example, can whiplash so that their flowers and leaves are lacerated by their own thorns. Perennials—even those that don't require staking—are blown over. Flowers can be wrenched right off the stems and after vicious storms, lawns and paths can be littered with an unseasonal debris of leaves torn off the trees while they are still green.

All this makes life hell for your plants. They survive, mostly, because they are naturally adaptable and tough, but they do not thrive and the garden gets a sad, tousled look where the overview may not be too bad but a walk round the borders will reveal ailing shrubs, damaged flowers and misshapen trees. Clearly, the most important task ahead is to do something about the wind.

Lack of shade
An exposed garden will be short of shade. This is not disastrous, but without it the numer of plants you can grow is far more limited. So many beautiful shrubs, trees and perennials prefer growing in shade that it would be a pity not to plan to create at least one darker corner. The very nature of shade is that it is usually sheltered too. Indeed, in some areas, the word

'shade' is used colloquially to mean shelter from wind as well as for cutting out direct sunlight. There are various ways in which this can be contrived – all to be described later – but it is mentioned here just to make you aware of its importance. Shade is also attractive because it enables you to introduce a further dimension to the garden. Walking through any well-designed garden, the visitor should experience changes in mood and emphasis. Some parts will be bright and colourful, others will be more subtle in their planting. However small the plot, these contrasts are not only perfectly possible but are highly desirable in order to create year-round variation and interest.

Effects of weather
Exposed gardens get the worst of the weather. Wind has already been discussed, but rain combined with wind can intensify the abuse of summer plants. In winter, the main problem is snow and high ground usually gets more. Where snow fall is gentle, the sheltered garden suffers more because the snow is more likely to stick to the branches of trees and bring them down. When snow is accompanied by winds and drifting takes place, the gar-

den is vulnerable for several reasons. First, in extreme cases, wind may blow most of the cover away from hilltop gardens. This is damaging if the temperature rapidly sinks because thick snow protects the ground and plant roots from the extremes of frost. Alternatively, the garden may be situated so that drifting occurs in the most inconvenient places. Apart from the misery of digging your way out of the front door, snowdrifts can squash plants or break off branches, so planting species with brittle wood in a snowdrift zone would be foolhardy. Anything with horizontal branches is particularly vulnerable to snow damage where drifting occurs, but fastigiate trees (those with branches that grow vertically) like Lombardy poplars or Irish yews, can splay out under the weight of sticky wet snow. All these problems can be minimized by thoughtful planting.

ASSESSING THE SITE

Having dismissed the main difficulties caused by exposed sites, the next step is to decide on the common problems affecting your own garden. In some gardens there may be no more than one windy corner, in others the whole area might be exposed. Each garden is individual with its own special characteristics. However, certain general problems are commonplace and need to be understood before they can be solved. But they *can* be solved – all of them – and once they are, you will no longer have an exposed garden. The secret of success is not to worry about the bad aspects of your site but to recognize and capitalize on the assets.

Brand new site
A new house often has a windy garden. Nothing is planted so there is nothing to restrict the wind. The problem is often compounded by poor soil or soil ruined by the builders. The first requirement here is to get rid of broken bricks and rubbish, assess the kind of soil you've inherited and start to work out a plan. Planting and design will be covered later, but at this stage we need to assess the situation and get to know what the conditions are really like.

Soil type
Having cleaned up the site, you must find out what type of soil you have. This is important because it will enable you to choose the kinds of plant that will be happiest in their surroundings. Planting

rhododendrons, for example, in chalky soil is an expensive waste of time because they will die. Clematis will refuse to thrive in thin sand and roses prefer heavy clay soils, although they're pretty tolerant of almost everything else.

The first thing you need to find out is your soil's acidity which is measured and expressed as pH. Technically, the definition of pH is: *the negative decimal logarithm of hydrogen ion concentration expressed in moles per litre.* You probably knew that already, but if you didn't, don't worry because all you need to know is that pH 7 is neutral. Anything less than pH 7 is acid and anything higher is alkaline. Therefore, if your soil reads pH 6.8 or less you can happily grow rhododendrons, but over about pH 7.2 they will not thrive. It is possible to buy a simple testing kit for pH from a garden centre, and once you have measured your soil you will be able to start compiling a list of suitable plants to grow. Little can be done to alter your soil's chemical characteristics, but there will always be a huge choice of different plants which will grow happily for you.

Other problems specific to your soil can often be sorted out. You cannot change sand to clay, but you can build it up by working in plenty of compost and manure and you can reduce the cold stickiness of clay by installing a drainage system. Grade one fertile loam might be essential for profitable crop farming, but is not necessary for the perfect garden. Indeed, in some respects it can be a positive handicap! Alpine gardeners and wildflower enthusiasts in lush farming areas have to go to great lengths to impoverish their soils to prevent their plants from growing too vigorously, so if you do not have perfect soil, do not despair.

Rainfall
Besides knowing about your garden soil, you should also have a rough idea of rainfall. As a general rule, the nearer you live to a western coast the damper it is. In the world's temperate regions prevailing winds tend to be westerly, and if they are coming straight to you from one of the great oceans, the chances are they'll also be carrying water. Nearer the tropics, the air tends to flow towards the east. In Australia, for example, land in the eastern states between the Great Dividing Range and the Pacific Ocean, gets plenty of rain but as you go west, it gets drier. As with

Even when cut to the ground by frost, buddleias soon regenerate. The variegated form Buddleia davidii 'Harlequin' has reddish purple flowers and attracts butterflies.

pH, your local rainfall will help to determine which plants will thrive in your garden.

Local wind

Local wind direction is also important. Where does it usually come from? Is it stronger at certain times of year? Is the area prone to squally storms from time to time or is there a nearly continuous airflow? Knowing these details will help you to achieve the best garden design. You may not find everything out at once – in fact you might have to live in one place for several years before you are able to understand or experience everything the weather can throw at you. But within a short time you will have gathered enough information to be able to make a fairly shrewd assessment of what to expect.

Certain areas have typical characteristics. As latitude increases, either north or south, the wind strength increases proportionally. England is therefore windier than Italy but more sheltered than Iceland. Coastal regions are more exposed to wind than inland areas and lowland is usually calmer than mountain areas.

Wind and temperature are important considerations. A hill-top town near the sea is probably windier than a low lying community inland, but will usually enjoy higher temperatures in winter. This could mean the difference between life and death for such invaluable plants as hebes or griselinias – both useful windbreak plants. The warm currents forming the Gulf Stream and North Atlantic Drift have an immense effect on the climate of Northern Europe, preventing places like northern Norway from becoming arctic wastelands and allowing gardens in the north west of Scotland to grow certain sub-tropical plants that would struggle to survive 20 degrees or more south in, say, West Virginia.

Many areas have local winds, resulting from the surrounding topography. These can be helpful – as in the case of the so-called Fremantle Doctor, bringing a refreshing sea breeze to Western Australia during heat waves – or catastrophic. The Mistral, for example, which whistles snow-cooled air down the Rhône valley keeps southern French gardeners on their toes. Most places have well known local quirks in the climate's general pattern and these will become familiar to you as you begin to understand your new garden.

Existing gardens with exposure problems

An attractive garden is never instant. Over the years seasoned experts groom their borders edging ever nearer perfection. For the rest of us, it's a case of putting the worst mistakes right as fast as they become obvious. Later we will deal with specific garden designs and plans, but making a clear assessment of the problems in hand at an early stage will enable us to put things right more effectively.

Most gardens, even the most thoughtfully planted, have a difficult corner. This could be a strip along the side of the house, or a sector that is prey to the worst of the wind. As with the new garden, it pays to study these trouble spots to find out what the problem is, where the wind comes from and what the symptoms are. If you identify the problem, you're halfway to solving it. Sometimes a difficult decision has to be made, particularly if a tree or a wall is in entirely the wrong place. Both can *increase* wind damage: a wall tends to stop the wind, causing it to eddy over the top, creating a billowing effect on the leeward side. A complete re-designing job may be the only solution, but often serious wind problems can be reduced by making small adjustments to the planting or minor alterations to the layout.

Living in a wind tunnel

This can prove to be the most alarming problem of all, and is often associated with town gardens. The explanation is simple: wind velocity is accelerated by forcing it through a narrowing gap. Therefore, wind blowing towards a row of houses will be funnelled through the spaces between them. Hillsides, quarry sides or banks will produce the same effect. This means that plants growing in the teeth of such winds have little chance of survival and at best will exist but not thrive. However, like other wind problems, most wind tunnels can be neutralized by combining temporary or permanent artificial barriers with strategic planting. The results of such measures are as dramatic as the wind damage was before and within a short time you will forget you ever had the problem.

Coastal sites

As we know, coastal areas are windy places. There is also the added problem of salt being carried on the wind. Most tender young foliage is inclined to scorch in rough weather because the wind contains salt water, which lands on the surface of the leaves and then evaporates, leaving a salt-deposit which is mildly caustic. Plants which grow wild near sea shores have leathery leaves or other protective devices so that this problem is reduced. The world is populated with a vast range of maritime and semi-maritime plants, including trees and shrubs, so that planning a seaside garden is simplicity itself. The problem is not what to plant but what to leave out. By creating a good salt-proof barrier, more susceptible species can then be introduced. Many seaside areas enjoy much milder winters, and if the garden is near an estuary the chances are that the soil will consist of a rich, fertile alluvial silt.

Hill tops

Hill sites are doubly exposed. Firstly, because they are high up, the wind speed is faster and gales are felt more intensely and secondly, at the summit a building and its surrounding garden are subjected to wind from all the points of the compass. Shelter is still possible, even up there, but it will take time to achieve and will probably need a little artificial help in the form of windbreaks or

Japanese quinces defy the wildest weather flowering in winter and spring. This variety, Chaenomeles speciosa *'Nivalis' is the purest white but there are many reds and pinks.*

other temporary barriers.

As far as soil is concerned, hilltops are the antithesis of flood plains or coastal silt-lands. In fact, the good soil that occurs in the lowlands has usually been eroded from the tops of the hills and washed down towards the sea. Hilltop fertility, there-fore, needs to be restored by adding plenty of nitrogen, potash and phosphorus sources. The soil condition and organic content must also be improved with plenty of compost, leafmould or rotted manure.

Many hill top gardens are rocky and this can be turned to advantage by designing a garden where alpine plants are featured. There are plenty of keen plantsmen who would love to have a naturally stony terrain in which to grow their treasures. You might even be lucky enough to have a little stream up there – a perfect opportunity to adjust its course so that it widens into pools and rills and creates small, sheltered spots for moisture-loving plants.

ADVANTAGES OF EXPOSED GARDENS

Before going into specific de-tails in the next chapter, it is worth making a note or two about the clear advantages of having an exposed garden.

Frost

Disastrous frosts are not usually those that fall in mid-winter. At that time of year, when temperatures are at their lowest, most plants are tucked up safely in a state of dormancy. In the northern states of North America and much of continental Europe most regions are under a pro-tective blanket of snow so that the air temperature be-comes more or less irrelevant to what is going on down below at root level. Frost be-comes a real bogeyman in late spring, because this is when daytime temperatures begin to rise and new growth is well under way. Keen gardeners concerned about their bud-ding plants listen to weather forecasts with anguish in their hearts. A still, sunny day can lead to a ground frost at night, particularly in shel-tered places. In calm condi-tions, cold dense air rolls downhill to gather in hollows of low-lying land until the temperature at ground level approaches freezing point. To make matters worse, foliage moisture evaporates and re-duces the temperature caus-ing ice crystals to form even though the surrounding temperature may be as much as 2°C (36°F). In exposed gardens, this is less likely to happen so, while your friends lower down are losing their magnolia flowers or the fresh shoots on their early potatoes, the slightest breeze is enough in your own garden to keep the frost off.

The effect of late frosts is made worse in sheltered gardens by the plants themselves. In a cold environment spring foliage is far more reluctant to emerge than in an area with a gentle climate. An hour or two of early spring sunshine will not make much of an impression on the exposed garden where spring buds will remain tightly furled until the days lengthen and become markedly warmer. In a sheltered valley, a south- or west-facing slope will act as a suntrap and early plants will rush into leaf only to be cut off in their prime the same night because of ground frost.

Light intensity

Sheltered gardens are often shady, which is an ideal condition for a wide range of plants, but not for vegetables. In some cases, such gardens can be given more light by removing some of the tree cover. Elsewhere, usually because of buildings, this is impossible. If you have an exposed, windy garden, the chances are there will be plenty of light. With careful placing of trees and other windbreaks, it will be possible not only to manufacture shaded areas, but also to ensure that parts of the garden continue to enjoy full light and can therefore grow sun-loving plants and vegetables. Variety, after all, is what will make the garden more interesting and more satisfying.

SUMMARY

1 Every garden plot, every bare site has both advantages and disadvantages. There is no such thing as an impossible or unworkable garden.

2 Wind is the main consideration. In order to convert an exposed garden into a sheltered one wind must be eliminated.

3 It is essential to get to know your site well by finding out it's soil type, local climate and other prevailing factors.

4 Coastal and hilltop gardens have their own special needs.

5 Exposed gardens have certain advantages, mainly more light and less late frost, which really should be exploited to the full.

BEATING THE WEATHER

In the first chapter we discussed the importance of getting to know the garden. Once you've found out the best facts, as well as the worst, about the site the next step is to decide how to make the most of the advantages and minimize the disadvantages. If it is worth doing at all, gardening is worth doing well. At the same time, it must never become a punishment or a chore. Better to concrete the whole thing over and take up hang gliding than to be tied to the millstone of an unloved garden! Of course, if you get the design and planting right you will find that you have the time to run a perfectly lovely garden and to go hang gliding as well.

Since wind is likely to be a major preoccupation at first, it is necessary to find a way of keeping it at bay. This is possible by erecting barriers, growing them or using a combination of the two. After a short time in a new garden, you will soon know where the coldest and most exposed spots are. From the start, this knowlege will influence your design.

Going for contrasting leaf colour, Cotinus coggygria *'Purpurea' and* Elaeagnus pungens *'Maculata' make a fine pair.*

TAKING STOCK OF NATURAL FEATURES

Wherever the site is positioned, there will be certain helpful features. The house itself will provide shelter to a sizeable area where the first of the more delicate plants can be planted. Inevitably, there will be a cool, shady side as well as a warmer, brighter zone, so you may choose to accentuate these differences with extra planting. There will often be existing walls and fences and perhaps some trees, which can be increased so that shelter can be built up gradually.

Neighbouring features will also influence your design and can often be beneficial. Street trees or neighbouring shrubberies can make excellent backdrops, especially if you have little of your own to enjoy. Buildings are a mixed blessing, they often exclude sunlight (not always a bad thing) but may cause destructive quirks in the wind. They may also provide valuable shelter, especially if they are constructed between your garden and the direction of the prevailing wind.

Hills, even if they are up to a mile away, exert some influence. Cold air has a nasty habit of rolling down a steep slope in still conditions, so land at the foot of the hill may be more susceptible to frost. Winds diverted round ranges of hills have a local effect in certain weather conditions. In my own village it is said that the hills to the west divert thunder storms and showers so that 12mm (½in) of desperately needed summer rain can fall a mile away while we watch the threatening clouds build up, but drift past us on the either side without shedding more than a momentary sprinkle. There is no scientific proof of this but local observation suggests that it is true.

Besides the possible functional advantages that local features may supply, we must also take stock of the way in which they might improve the garden. The whole point of gardening, besides growing some of the food we eat and having somewhere to relax at the weekend, is to enjoy the visual effect. Make no mistake, gardening is as much an art form as painting or sculpture except that everyone has the ability to do it and can achieve impressive results with minimal skills. So, having assessed your site for the various physical features such as soil type, existing structures, climate and so on, you must now decide whether there is any artistic merit already evident. What can you see from the sitting room window? Where does the front gate lead to? Is that scrubby hawthorn bush too far gone to rescue or might it make a central point for a new mixed border?

Above all, you will have to take the views or vistas into consideration. As we have discussed, an open panorama with the vision unobstructed for miles will guarantee a windy garden. But if it is spectacular, it would be a shame to eliminate it by erecting a high fence or by planting a row of evergreens. There is a number of ways in which a compromise can be reached and these will be covered on pages 44 – 46 but it *is* a compromise and it must not be forgotten that to create sheltered conditions a good deal of the panorama will have to be sacrificed. It's a matter of choice.

ARTIFICAL STRUCTURES

The quickest way to take action against the wind is to put up some kind of barrier. Walls are permanent, plastic-net screens are temporary. Woven-larch fences are supposed to be permanent, but are disappointingly short-lived, especially if the posts have not been installed prop-erly. Plastic-net screening, temporary though it is, can be a first rate wind-shield, parti-cularly for young trees. Here are some examples of effective windbreaks from the most temporary to the most perma-nent. Naturally, the cost tends to rise in proportion with the degree of perma-nence.

Screening materials
These are the least attractive but are often more effective than anything else. The point about them is that they let the wind pass through them, but reduce its speed. This means that there are no des-tructive eddy currents on their leeward sides. One of the crudest and simplest types is loose-woven hessian (burlap). It can be purchased from an agricultural mer-chant by the roll – usually 50 m (55 yd) – and its natural beige colour fades as it weath-ers. It should be fixed to up-right posts set at no more than 3 m (10 ft) intervals. Strips of wood about 12 mm (½ in) thick and at least 25 mm (1 in) wide should be nailed to the posts, sand-wiching the hessian to hold it secure. One, two or three lengths of wire stretched taut-ly between the posts will help to prevent the hessian from billowing and flapping about.

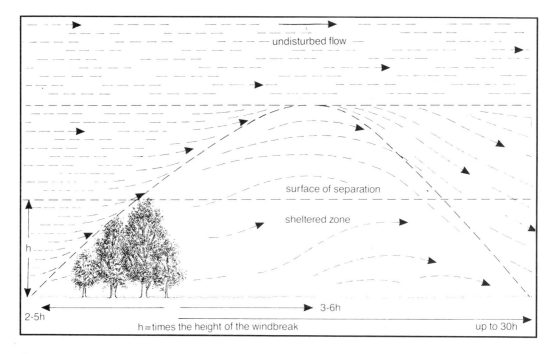

undisturbed flow

surface of separation

sheltered zone

h

2-5h

3-6h

h=times the height of the windbreak

up to 30h

Fig. 1. Semipermeable windbreaks, as opposed to solid barriers, slow down the rate of the wind without causing damaging eddy currents.

Within three years the material will begin to rot and disintegrate, but by then the young trees it was protecting, will have become well established.

Plastic netting, though not pretty, is longer lasting and equally effective. There are several brands, which have been specifically developed as windbreak material on the market nowadays. In horticulture and agriculture it has many uses, from keeping wind off apple orchards, to sheltering new-born lambs in early spring. Black seems to be the most widely available colour and will be less obtrusive in the garden than any other. Because it is so effective in slowing down wind velocity – this netting acts like a leaky sail – it exerts considerable pressure on the supporting posts. If timber ones are used these should be no further apart than about 3 m (10 ft) but for badly exposed positions, metal uprights might be safer to use. Old scaffolding poles have proved useful to me in this respect. Set these into concrete poured into holes at least 60 cm (2 ft) deep. Angle iron, provided it is of a heavy enough gauge, is almost as good and has the advantage of being easier to drill and bolt than rounded scaffolding poles.

Other wind screening material is available from time to time. Long-lasting woven birch panels are attractive, especially as they weather and grow an encrustation of lichens. Woven coconut fibre or coir has been traditionally used in Kentish hop gardens but is heavy and rough on the skin.

Fences

A well-constructed fence is attractive and easy on the eye but so many are bodged together and in varying states of collapse. Since wood is the most popular material, and this is frequently preserved with chemicals which are toxic to plants, it is difficult to get climbers to thrive on the fence. Then, when they do finally get established they usually rot the fence and the whole thing falls down.

Faulty posts are the most common cause of failure. Softwood posts have a short life, especially when hammered directly into the ground. Set in concrete they do last a little longer but water tends to collect at the point where they disappear into the surface and this is where they most frequently rot and snap. Special metal holders with sharp points that hammer into the ground are available but still do not prevent rotting. Hard-wood posts are expensive but last much longer, proving the point – you get what you pay for!

The same rule applies to the panels. Woven softwood is fine in the short term but does not last more than a few years without beginning to go shabby. Flexing and bending in the wind, the upright sections begin to shift and after that the woven strips work loose and holes begin to appear. Lapped softwood is more expensive and is said to be artistic but looks as cheap and nasty to me as does woven larch. Hardwood panelling looks beautiful but is very expensive. Victorian style trellis, densely constructed, can be both artistic and functional, especially when adorned with interesting climbers. But such trellis is also expensive and you will find that it does not last as long as hardwood panelling.

The choice depends not only on cost but on the fence's position. If it is to form a boundary, there is little point in spending too much money on it. If, on the other hand, you wish to construct a decorative screen in an important position, choose the best materials you can afford. You won't regret it. Besides lasting longer they will look much more attractive.

Walls

Few gardens are built with extensive walls these days because of the enormous cost of materials and labour. Building a wall is much easier than most people think but is very time consuming. Provided the foundations are firm and level, the rest is straightforward if you work at a leisurely pace, measuring up and using a plumb-line regularly to make sure your brick, stone or block laying is level and vertical. There are plenty of useful books on brick and block work but one point they all miss out is that it is far easier to install vine eyes or supporting pegs as you build. Later, when the cement is dry, you can thread them with wire so that climbing plants will be easy to train.

Mellow brick—preferably about 400 years-old—or honey-coloured sandstone are about the nicest building materials to use. That is why wisterias and rambling roses look so good on the walls of ancient monuments! Few of us are lucky enough to have such materials but secondhand stone and brick can be found and is well worth hoarding. Modern concrete blocks are the easiest to work with and will mellow, eventually. However, since they are rather ugly at first, the sooner they can be completely overgrown with climbers the better. But do not be tempted to use rampant weeds such as *Polygonum baldschuanicum* (Russian vine) since this will swamp everything and ruin the garden. If local planning rules allow, build as high as you can. A 2.1 m (7 ft) wall provides more shelter than one at 1.5 m (5 ft) and will give you more vertical space on which to grow plants.

Pre-cast concrete blocks of openwork design, create screens but allow a certain amount of light and air through. They need very careful siting in private gardens to avoid a somewhat tawdry look.

LIVING SCREENS

Living screens can be used in conjunction with artificial barriers or can replace them altogether. Usually they look more attractive but they always take longer to establish themselves and, while you are waiting for this to happen, there may be little to stop the wind.

Hedges

What could be finer than a well-established beech hedge? Hedges have been popular in gardens for centuries which is hardly surprising because few

cultural techniques have so
ably combined usefulness
with ornament. There is
nothing quite so effective
against wind as a well-grown
hedge. There are so many
different species of woody
plant that lend themselves to
hedging that some are worth
growing just as interesting
features. At Kiftsgate Court,
in Gloucestershire, England,
a *Rosa gallica* 'Versicolor'
(Rosa Mundi) hedge has been
planted and every midsum-
mer is awash with large fragrant, striped roses. The 17th-
century diarist John Evelyn
had a superb 400 ft holly
hedge which was ruined by
Tsar Peter the Great during a
house visit. He and his horse
used it for jumping practice —
poor hedge! Poor horse!

Hedges develop quite
quickly provided they are
planted in ideal conditions.
The trouble with exposed gardens is that growing conditions are probably not ideal
and so a temporary screen,
however ugly, may be needed
to protect the young hedge
while it develops. The secret
of successful hedge establish-
ment lies in first developing a
thick bottom. The most common fault is to allow the
growth to reach the hedge's
desired height quickly without worrying too much about
the bases of the hedging

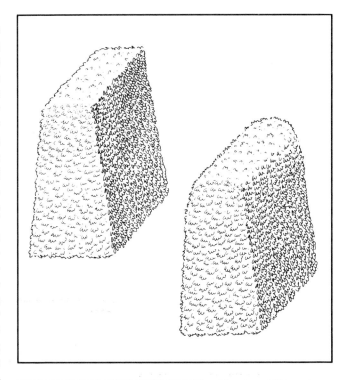

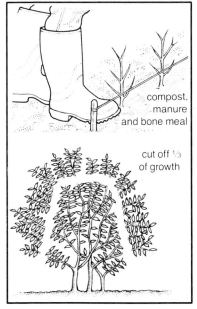

compost,
manure
and bone meal

cut off 1/3
of growth

Fig. 2. a. Different
hedge shapes. Always
try to ensure hedge is
wider at bottom than
at top.
b. Plant in trenches or
holes which are big
enough to
accommodate the root
system. Tread plants
firmly in.
c. Prune at least one
third of growth back as
soon as planting is
complete.

plants. Cutting very hard back straight after planting—at least one-third of the overall height—will help to ensure maximum branching of each hedging plant from near the ground upwards.

During its formative years the hedge can be cut back quite firmly once a year, preferably in mid July, regardless of how much it has grown. How much you cut off depends on how quickly it is growing into shape but it's essential to have a firm outline in your mind. At first, only a small part of the hedge will have reached the necessary dimensions but gradually holes and gaps will fill out and symmetry will be reached. Cutting in a wedge shape, wider at the bottom than the top, will ensure healthy growth and make the hedge more weather-proof. The rate of growth varies from season to season but good planting conditions are essential for establishing a dense, uniform hedge.

How to plant a hedge
1 Mark out the line your hedge will take. Garden design will be covered on pages 40-57, so for our purpose here, we will assume you know exactly where the hedge will be. Work out exactly how many plants you'll need. (Plant spacings are given in point 4 below).
2 Select your hedge species and then go about acquiring the plants. The merits of different hedges will be covered shortly but, whatever you choose, always go to a reputable nursery or garden centre. If you buy by mail order—a useful system—be sure to inspect the plants on arrival. Any doubts about them should be reported to the suppliers *at once* and inferior stock returned. The roots of your transplants must never be allowed to dry out.
3 Prepare the ground. If the soil is good, all you need do is dig a trench about 30 cm (1 ft) deep and wide enough to accommodate the roots of the hedging plants. Sprinkle some bonemeal [about 30 gm (1oz) for each plant] into the bottom and mix with the soil. In poor or rocky soil, proceed as above but remove any stones and dig down to 45 cm (1½ ft). Into this trench, mix in bonemeal (same rate as before) and well-rotted manure, leafmould or compost. The object is to increase the organic content of the soil; to step up fertility; to improve its water-retaining properties and hence, to boost early growth.
4 Plant the hedge, spacing the young plants 45 cm (18 in)

apart [conifers 90 cm (3 ft) apart], firming the roots in well. In extremely exposed sites, the plants can be staggered at 30 cm (1 ft) intervals but in most gardens, lining them up straight at 45 cm (18 in) intervals is perfectly adequate. In badly exposed areas, the plants can be supported with canes or by suspending a wire tautly between posts at either end and tying each to the wire. Make sure all ties are loose enough to allow for stem thickening and remove all supports within three years. If you are worried about cost and are prepared to wait slightly longer for the hedge to thicken, increase the spacing to 60 cm (2 ft).

5 Take your courage and your secateurs firmly in your hand and cut at least one third of the growth off NOW! If you bought 90 cm (3 ft) plants, none of them should be taller than 60 cm (2 ft) within an hour of planting. Note: this does not apply to conifers which should be left untrimmed until well established.

Aftercare is simple: prevent weeds from growing in the hedge bottom for a year or two while the growth thickens. In the first year, water the hedge copiously in dry weather. That means a good soak every three weeks rather than a daily sprinkle.

I like to feed new hedges each spring for their first few years, using a compound that contains 15% each of nitrogen, phosphorus and potash plus trace elements. A dessertspoonful is plenty for each plant. Beech, hornbeam, most flowering hedges, yew and holly will get by with a single annual clip. Privet, *Lonicera nitida* and hedges in sub-tropical areas will need clipping more than once each year.

The choice

Choice of hedge material depends on your preferences and on what it is being used for. Purely decorative hedges can be flowery and informally clipped. *Rosa rugosa* cultivars have the ability to regulate their own height, according to conditions, and produce an abundance of fragant blossoms followed by colourful autumn hips. For more severe formality, the traditional material is *Taxus baccata* (yew) and with good reason. It is tough, easy to trim, only needs attention once a year, makes a dark foil to contrast with brighter flowers and foliage and, contrary to popular belief, is quite a fast grower. The disadvantages with yew are that it is extremely poisonous to livestock, especially horses, and that it makes such a dense cover that plants underneath have a hard time surviving at all. Furthermore, yew can be boring, it is virtually the same colour throughout the year.

Some deciduous hedges, if properly trimmed, keep their brown leaves all winter. *Fagus sylvatica* (beech) is popular and, once established, makes a superb hedge and a perfect windbreak. In heavier soils, *Carpinus betulus* (hornbeam) is better than beech but has similar habits. The variations in colour through the year are entertaining— beige in late winter, emerald young foliage breaking through this in mid spring, sombre green in summer just when other colours in the garden are at their most riotous and then a gentle decline into autumn gold. Beech leaves, both purple and green varieties, are rich tan in winter, hornbeam is soft beige. There's much to be said for both.

Wildlife enthusiasts may like to introduce rough shelter belts or tapestry hedges. These can be composed of selections of native plants or mixtures of natives and exotics. The process of making a garden more sheltered will inevitably lead to an increase in wildlife population so, if this is to be enhanced and expanded, the guests should be supplied with what they need. Foodplants for butterfly larvae, nesting sites for birds, nectar plants for bees and other insects, and refuge areas for reptiles and amphibians can all be supplied within an established hedge, which will still look beautiful, regardless of its 'weed' content. Clipping here is a matter of convenience. Some pruning is essential to promote thick, branching shrubs which will stay wind-proof but, whether this is annual or less frequent depends on how much space you want the hedge to take up. Remember to clip *after* bird nesting has finished, or before it begins.

Flowering hedges, besides the roses mentioned earlier, make colourful barriers, but the more you clip the less they flower. Species which have but one flowering season, such as lilacs, *Ribes sanguineum*, or mock orange, should be pruned back as soon as the flowers have faded. This will ensure maximum growth before the next flowering season but will also tend to make for long, lax stems which are less good at keeping out the weather. Pruning later, in mid summer, is a good compromise.

Since the end of World War II there has been an abiding obsession with conifers. The crossing of two genera to produce the fabled × *Cupressocyparis leylandii* was a mixed blessing. Few trees are finer for screening large areas, not only from wind, but also from sight. However, the proliferation of outsize hedges in tiny suburban gardens have, quite rightly, caused a backlash against the mighty Leyland cypress. If there is room use this plant for your screen but remember, that in the right conditions, it will attain a height of 3 m (10 ft) in five years. Furthermore, being naturally shallow rooted, it will deprive all adjacent soil of moisture and nutrients, creating a harsh environment for other plants. In small gardens, slower conifers can be clipped into stately hedges just as easily and will not rob the soil so much. For mild areas, one of the Leyland's parents, *Cupressus macrocarpa*, makes an altogether charming hedging plant, especially the bright gold-green clone 'Goldcrest'.

So, in order of 'windproofness' and 'hardiness' your choice runs from yew, holly, beech and hornbeam through to the laurels, *Prunus laurocerasus* and *Prunus lusitanica* (both rather dour evergreens). Alternatively choose the conifers like Lawson cypress, *Chamaecyparis lawsoniana*, or one of the many decorative clones, flowering shrubs like escallonias, lilacs, roses, cotoneasters, pyracanthas and finally, as a last choice, privet and lonicera. It all depends on how much space you have, how bad the winds are and your own personal likes and dislikes.

Trees

Besides hedges you'll need some good-sized trees, partly for shelter and partly because few gardens look right without them. When designing and laying out a new garden, trees become central focal points around which the rest of the planting takes shape. In exposed gardens the object of much of the tree planting may well be to afford shelter and for no other reason. However, since the trees will have to be looked at as well as keeping the wind off, you might as well make the best selections to suit not only your conditions but also your taste.

The shelter belt

The idea of the shelter belt is to separate your precious garden plants from the elements. Farmers, in the days when

good husbandry prevailed, planted them to protect livestock from the wind and to provide cover for game. In a small garden, planting a shelter belt of forest trees is out of the question—there just isn't enough room. In an open-plan system of gardens, limited co-operative planting could take place, but in a medium or large private garden, setting aside a belt several yards thick along the length of the windward side for trees could change the environment within.

The procedure is not unlike that for a hedge, except that you will be planting individual trees and shrubs in groups rather than in a straight or curving line. Different species can be used, and since the area taken up is likely to be quite large in relation to the rest of the garden, you might as well choose trees and shrubs which will contribute differently throughout the year. In fact there need never be a dull period—holly berries at Christmas, cherry blossom in the spring, fragrant shrub roses in high summer, russet foliage in autumn and so on. Plant everything closely at first, and then as the forest grows up, be prepared to thin out up to half the original numbers to give the rest some

fighting room. The ideal shelterbelt for a medium-sized garden is, in effect, a mixed border with a high 'centre of gravity'. For quick height you could plant maples such as *Acer saccharum* (sugar maple), *Populus tremula* (quaking aspen), and perhaps even the speedy Hungarian oak, *Quercus frainetto*. Smaller trees could include any of the sorbus species, especially the orange berried 'Joseph Rock' or the pink berried *S. hupenhensis;* flowering apples such as *Malus* 'Hillieri' (pink); cherries, especially white ones or *Prunus sargentii* which has such good autumn colour. You'll also need some evergreen trees, particularly *Ilex aquifolium* (holly) cultivars and, if mild enough, *Eucryphia cordifolia* (late summer flowering) or camellias which flower in the spring.

These larger specimens would be underplanted with a range of interesting smaller shrubs and the spaces between them crammed with herbaceous plants like lilies, pulmonarias, primroses, spring and autumn bulbs and so on. Getting the idea? After a few years, when the area is becoming congested, the populus and some of the big maples could be weeded out along with half the smaller

This Escallonia bifida *has attracted Painted Lady, Red Admiral, Comma and Small Tortoiseshell butterflies. It needs the protection of a wall in frosty areas.*

shrubs, leaving behind the more choice plants which will have taken longer to establish themselves. Over the years, the gaps can be filled and plants you've begun to dislike replaced with more treasured items—that is the art of gardening.

On the cheap

The shelter belt just described will be expensive to plant, but a similar effect can be obtained more cheaply by using more commonplace plants and choosing smaller trees. Large standard specimens cost a great deal of money and, unless the aftercare is meticulous, can languish for years before they make up their minds about whether to live or die. Small saplings or 'whips' with just a single main stem, grow away quickly and will overtake transplanted standards within a decade.

For large projects, where woodland planting is contemplated, a hundred small saplings can be purchased from a wholesaler at the same cost as five standard trees from the garden centre.

Planting technique

Trees are easy to plant. The rules for ground preparation are exactly as described in the section on hedges (see pages 28-33). The vital requirement is to stake them correctly. Local authority tree planting is normally based on the old fashioned idea that a standard tree should have at least one long pole next to it with two or even three ties holding it securely—the top one looking more like a device for garrotting than an aid for survival! This is probably as much to deter vandalism as to support the tree. In private gardens, all that matters is to hold the root rigid in the ground but to let the stem of the tree flex in the wind. This causes it to thicken into a trunk quickly and the tree to grow at a faster rate than with a long stake. Short stakes must be very strong because there will be considerable leverage on them so, although no more than 45 cm (18 in) may be showing above the ground, there should be as much as 60 cm (2 ft) below. Short stakes can be removed after two growing seasons in most cases.

If newly planted trees fail, two main causes are likely: (a) the roots drying out before planting and, (b) inadequate water supply in the first two years of growth. If the small, fibrous roots dry, the microscopic root hairs are killed off and the plant can no longer draw water into its system. All transplanting is unnatural and some damage is unavoidable. Therefore, watering is essential during the period when the tree is repairing its root system. This is doubly important in exposed gardens where winds increase the evaporation rate.

IMPROVING THE SUBSTRATE

Most of this chapter has been concerned with planting the garden to make it sheltered. Before moving onto specific designs in the next, we should first consider our substrate—the ground in which we are growing the plants. Being exposed and windy means an extra challenge to the plants, especially at first, while they are fighting to get established. Besides erecting temporary barriers and other devices to minimize the effect of the wind, we should also make sure that the soil is in as good a condition as possible.

Fertility
Poor soil will do nothing for the plants. Building up adequate reserves of the essential minerals is a simple matter and any serious deficiency can be put right quickly. Using natural manures is doubly beneficial because, as well as supplying minerals, they also build up the organic content. Soil contains billions of living micro-organisms which work away at releasing nitrogen for the green plants to use. Slow-release organic fertilizers such as blood meal, fish meal and bonemeal applied in the spring help to build up the big three elements—N.P.K. (nitrogen, phosphorus and potassium). They also go some way towards adding the elements needed in smaller quantities – magnesium, iron, cobalt, copper, manganese and others. Artificial fertilizer is equally effective and less unpleasant to use. When spreading organic dry fertilizers, watch for hygiene. There may not be much anthrax about these days but blood or bonemeal can carry plenty of other pathogens.

Moisture
You must aim to keep soil moist but freely drained in your garden. Raising organic content helps enormously, not only to build some body into the light soils but, oddly enough, to lighten heavy clay soils and make them more workable.

Drainage is vital. If water does not drain away naturally, it will be necessary to install under drainage in the form of a rubble underlay or

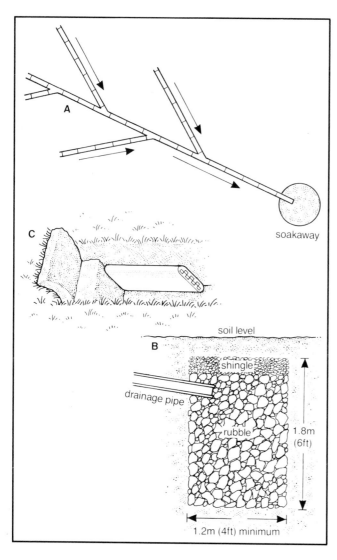

A

soakaway

C

soil level

B

shingle

drainage pipe

rubble

1.8m
(6ft)

1.2m (4ft) minimum

Fig. 3. Drainage systems: a. herringbone formation and c. narrow pipes laid in slit trenches. b. The main pipe must lead to a soakaway.

where they belong. Spent mushroom compost, old rotted manure, Irish moss peat and homemade garden compost all work well. Gradually, the mulch is 'eaten' up by the soil which is no bad thing, improving the top soil as it is absorbed.

Structure
Light, sandy soils have little structure. Dig out a spadeful in damp weather, drop it on top of the ground and it breaks up instantly into crumbly fragments. Nevertheless, it drains freely and is easy to work. Heavier loam, given the same treatment, stays the same shape and crumbles more reluctantly. Clay, however, can be moulded like putty. The heavier soils have a structure which can be damaged. The worst treatment is to work them when they are not dry enough. You may make a lovely tilth on the surface with your rake and fork in spring but, unless they are dry enough lower down, you could be paddling the subsoil into a hard pan through which neither roots nor water can run. On a brand new site, the builders are sure to have ruined your soil structure, so remedial action will be needed. Deep, double digging should do the trick, leaving

porous drain pipes to take surplus water away.

Further moisture loss can be slowed down by using thick mulches of organic material. Bark chips are in vogue these days, but are horrible to look at except in woodland gardens the clods on the surface for the winter frosts to break down into a tilth. Once the structure has been restored, take care not to spoil it again – keep off it until dry.

Now that we have looked at the various ways in which we can devise shelter for the garden, the next step is to look at some specific designs which will put these sound ideas into practice.

Summary

1   Start your plan by weighing up local features and any special qualities your garden may have. Look at any existing trees and plants, deciding whether these will fit in with your schemes or not.

2   Plan to construct artificial windbreaks while the new plants become established. Any wall building will be easier at this stage before the planting is done.

3   Consider what hedges to plant, matching up species you use to the garden's special conditions and to suit your own preferences.

4   Think about tree costs before opting for expensive standards. Whips grow faster and are much cheaper.

5   Give plenty of attention to the soil. Make sure drainage is adequate; build up organic content; hoard composting material – be a thrifty and conscientious steward of the land.

Mahonia aquifolium. *Quite the toughest flowering shrub known to man but pretty with its yellow flowers and dark fruits.*

SPECIAL CASES

Now that we have looked at general factors which determine what shape the garden will take, let's examine some specific situations to see how we can take advantage of the good points, but minimize the unfavourable ones. Obviously, every site is unique with its own exclusive characteristics but when you look through the next few pages you should recognize several aspects which are similar to your own plot or which, at the very least, strike a chord.

PROBLEMS

Each problem can be solved in dozens of ways and what follows here are merely suggestions offering various solutions. They don't need to be followed slavishly but are intended to stimulate your thoughts about your own garden and, hopefully, will inspire you to artistry. Assuming you have the land at your disposal – no matter how small or large an area – all you need now is a smattering of knowledge about plants and some self confidence. The joy of gardening is that, whatever age you start, you can learn as you go along and even as a beginner you can still achieve really impressive results.

Let's look now at some examples of windy gardens.

NEW SITES

Garden with good views in the heart of the wind.

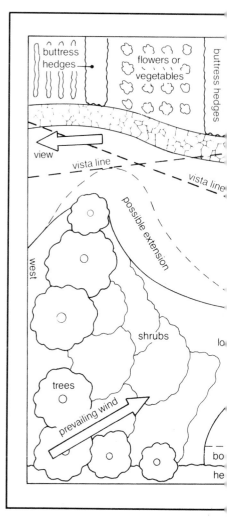

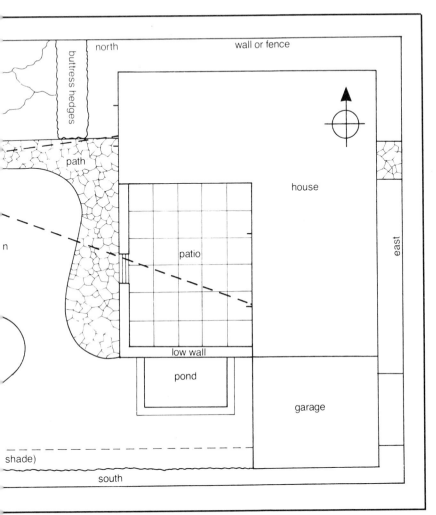

north

buttress hedges

wall or fence

path

house

patio

east

n

low wall

pond

garage

shade)

south

Fig. 4. a (Left). Organizing wind breaks but keeping the view. A sight line has been kept leading from the patio and house window to the outside but most of the garden is sheltered by tall plants and trees.
b (Below). Side view of buttress hedges showing gradual reduction in height towards the front of the border.

The plan shows the back garden only. Since the worst of the wind is from the southwest here, the front will tend to be nicely sheltered by the house and garage so need not concern us. The builders and architects have designed the best rooms to look out over stupendous views across glo-

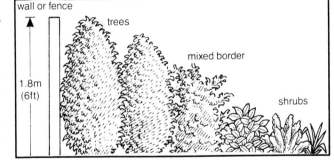

wall or fence

trees

mixed border

shrubs

1.8m (6ft)

rious country scenery. Alas, the area does get horrific gales every other month from exactly the same quarter. The dilemma is how much view to sacrifice and how much garden to protect.

The solution is to compromise. We'll assume that the house is modern and well insulated so wind blowing onto its west wing won't make much difference to the indoor temperatures or cause any draughts. Optimistically, the builders laid a patio within the 'L' shape of the building but the garden furniture you put there kept blowing over, proving that it was hardly an environment in which to sit happily sipping cool drinks. The logical plan is to shelter the patio area and the land to the south and west but to create a vista which opens onto the view of the landscape due west. Views to the south-west will be lost but shelter for most of the garden is gained.

Along the south boundary, a hedge should be planted. Since this is near the patio, it needs to look attractive, particularly in the summer months, and, because it is south of the garden, should be just high enough to ensure privacy and shelter without

Apple scented Geranium macrorrhizum *makes a colourful ground cover beneath the variegated form of* Weigela florida.

A happy association for autumn: Picea pungens *(blue spruce) contrasts with ripe stems of* Stipa gigantea.

blocking out too much sunshine. Any hedging material which lends itself to formal clipping will do – yew, hornbeam or beech, for example – or perhaps a mixture of species to create a pleasing tapestry effect. Flowering hedges or informal screen plants might not be suitable here because space is at a premium and you will want to clip to exact dimensions.

In front of the hedge there is room for a strip border, bearing in mind that when the hedge is fully grown this will be in dry shade. Moisture lovers like hostas or astilbes would hate it here, but there are plenty of alternatives. Several violet species are tough and vigorous for spring colour and foliage, looking good planted with small bulbs like scillas and chionodoxa. Later, these could give way to epimediums and small ferns, a foxglove or two for early summer colour and a further selection of summer flowers to follow. A pleasing alternative, especially if space is at a premium, is to have a single strip of one plant species set right at the hedge bottom, preferably selected to contrast well with the foliage of the hedge. Catmint is often used for this purpose and can flower reasonably well even in the shade. The blue goes well with sombre evergreens like yew or purple-leaved beech.

Moving west on the diagram, that corner is where the worst of the weather comes. Trees will be needed here, the type and size depending on the soil type and the size of the garden. It is along this stretch and round the corner to about half the length of the west side, that a temporary wind barrier, as described in pages 75-7, will help while the trees and shrubs are getting really established. In an isolated site bordering farmland, you can use cheap materials like hessian. It won't matter if this looks rather untidy for a year or so, but if you have close neighbours, go for a more expensive, neater material. If space is restricted, large shrubs can be used at the back instead of trees. Dreary though they are on their own, cherry and Portugal laurels make effective windbreaks and are reasonably fast growing. On acid soils the choice of evergreens extends to rhododendrons. The larger species grow quite fast, but some can develop naked limbs and need furnishing with smaller relatives down below. Further, some rhododendron species dislike too much wind and the toughest, *Rhododendron ponticum* is an invasive thug.

The high plants should continue along the western boundary to about two-thirds its length. Any less will make the garden too windy; much more will blot out too much of

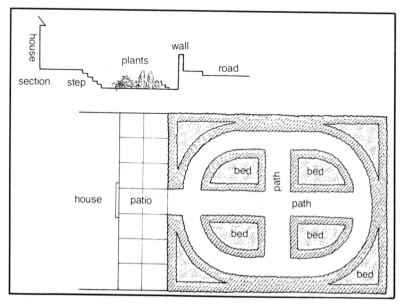

Fig. 5. a. Sectional view of a sunken garden where extra shelter has been contrived by raising a wall and lowering ground level within the enclosure.
b. A traditional knot garden where low hedges can provide shelter for small plants growing between them.

the view. Check up on your sight lines from the patio and the windows of the house to ensure that more than mere glimpses of the view remain. With care, the planting can also be arranged so that the patio receives the last few glorious rays of the evening sun as well as plenty of mid-day warmth.

If there is room, a small bower or little open space could be arranged on the west side of the mixed border, perhaps with a garden seat so that the panorama can be enjoyed there on calm days.

To the north of the garden is another border, or rather collection of borders, divided by buttress hedges.

Buttress hedges

These provide a perfect oppor-tunity to combine a useful function with art. Dividing up gardens into small spaces can make them more interesting and enjoyable to wander through. The buttress hedge has been used for many years in English gardens to very good effect. We'll assume that the boundary to the north consists of a wall – perhaps of another building – or even a fence. This is fine for privacy but will do nothing to protect the garden from the prevail-ing wind which will tend to blow along it. Hedges planted at right angles to the wall will break up the wind and reduce the eddy effect caused by the back wall. They will also cre-ate a series of little enclosures with a pattern of cosy en-vironments within. In a small garden, these may be less than 3 m (10 ft) square but will still have room to accommodate a broad selec-tion of colours and textures. The hedges should be as tall as possible at the back and slope down towards the front. The back wall or fence can be planted with climbers such as roses or clematis. Com-plementary shrubs, her-baceous plants and even alpines can then make up the planting in front, the height reducing gradually towards the front.

Similar enclosurers are per-fectly suitable for vegetables – kitchen gardens need not be ugly. Neatness, careful posi-tioning of the rows or blocks and keeping the plants heal-thy is essential. Replace gaps quickly, with quick-flowering annuals if not with more vegetables, as this will help to keep things looking pretty as well as functional. There are even colourful and attractive varieties of certain food plants although my own inclination is always to go for optimum flavour and yield, regardless of colour or shape. Runner

Opposite: Finest of the named Rosa rugosa *cultivars, 'Roseraie de l'Haÿ', whose winy purple flowers are richly scented and recurrent.*

beans, most herbs, seakale, tomatoes, aubergines and chard are all beautiful plants in their own right and belong anywhere in a well-planted garden.

A stone, gravel or crazy paving path along the front of the buttress border will enable you to bring the height of the plants down to a few inches and encourage them to spill over and seed themselves into the cracks. Paths often look better if their harsh lines are broken up this way.

Isolated hilltop

For the sake of variety, we will assume that this is a larger garden than the last. Few sites could be more challenging to the gardener than a bleak hilltop – although there is a cliffside garden in Derbyshire, England, I know of where the owner lowers herself down on a rope to do the weeding. There is no natural shelter anywhere so no matter which way the wind blows, the summit bears the brunt, always with more

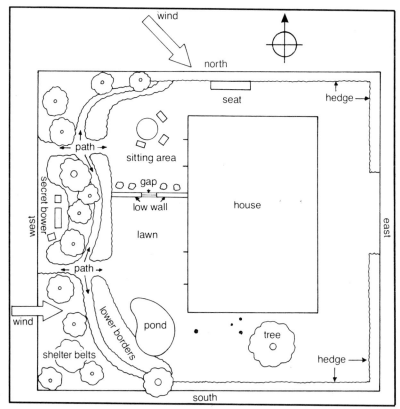

Right: Fig. 6. Surrounding a hilltop house with sheltering material. Note the gaps left for enjoying views and the outside 'bower' for sitting on calm days. Here, the gaps are opposite the windows so that some view is kept, even from the house.

intensity than anywhere else.

The only way effective shelter can be achieved here is to plant quite heavily on the perimeter. A thick shelter belt will be needed to windward but elsewhere, good, high hedges will leave more room for the garden. At first, it looks from the illustration as though most of the acreage is to be sacrificed to a batch of boring trees. However, the shelter belt itself will become one of the main and most beautiful features on the premises. The most urgent task will be to get the trees and shrubs established. As discussed on pages 33-7, they'll be thickly planted at first, but later, the faster growers can be removed to make way for the more classy specimens. Because of the likelihood of good views, gaps leading to the outside and even a secret bower can be arranged on the windward side for use on calm days. If the view is ugly, go for maximum protection and leave no gaps. Pathways leading through the middle of the shelter belt may seem a little unnecessary at first but within a few years can become charming woodland walks lined with primroses, oxlips, hellebores and daffodils in spring, Turk's cap lilies, monkshoods and blue poppies in summer, cyclamen in au-tumn and snowdrops and aconites in winter. Meanwhile, overhead trees and shrubs will produce catkins, blossoms, fruit and golden foliage in their seasons.

Within the garden, now enclosed by the shelter belt and hedges, there are thousands of possibilities. Once the shelter has grown up, you will be able to widen your range of plants considerably. The natural move might be to lay borders out along the inner edges of the shelter belt or under the hedges. This will look fine but a path separating the two will make it easier to service the borders from both sides and help to prevent weeds spreading from the shelter belt to the more manicured borders.

There will also be room for sitting areas, lawn and whatever other garden features you may wish to install. Since hilltop soil is usually poor, if you want a kitchen garden you'll need to work hard on improving the fertility. Pick the most well-lit part of the garden and keep building up the organic content of the soil by incorporating compost or manure. Fertility is not something that improves instantly. It takes several seasons during which the organic content gradually increases as well as essential minerals.

A small but exposed plot
6m (20ft) square or less
For the plot, say 6 m (20 ft) square or less two solutions spring to mind here. Part of my own front garden was open to the north-east and horribly exposed. Since it sloped slightly I decided to create two level terraces. The bottom one, even though only 60 cm (2 ft) lower than the other, is surprisingly sheltered, especially at ground level where the young emerging plants are most vulnerable. It is not often possible to go excavating to a very great extent, especially where neighbours are concerned, but a natural slope can usually be terraced to good effect. Looking out of the window onto a sunken area can be more aesthetic than seeing a slope fall away. The terracing helps to accentuate the level difference between top and bottom.

Plant height can be kept low, partly to minimize possible wind damage and partly to enhance the impression of a sunken site. Gardens of this kind look good from above as well as at ground level, which is another good reason for concentrating on low, carpeting plants. We covered the upper terrace of our sunken garden with pea-sized grit and planted a collection of helianthemums (rock roses) and dwarf iris hybrids there. The lower level is planned strictly for colour using golden foliage and cream, yellow and orange flowers. These shades are contrasted with deep blues and, as a result of careful selection, there are flowers of both colour groups on show for ten months of the year.

The second possibility is to borrow a page or two from the history books and construct a knot garden using a pattern of low hedges. Gardeners planted these all over the western world in the 16th century. There is no need to plan a design as complicated as some of the Elizabethan patterns, but a simple cross design with rounded corners will provide eight tiny beds for plants. Allowing the hedge material to grow to about 45 cm (18 in) will ensure protection for the plants within. There is no need to stick religiously to historic plants although box, the favourite material in Shakespeare's day, is easily the best for the hedging. In each little bed, choose one rose, ideally a small, richly scented type (preferably a pink china rose) to go with the bottle green box – and surround this with low plants of dwarf lavender, pansies, pinks or any other

little plants that give plenty of flower and contrasting foliage without taking up too much space. Spring bulbs can be fitted in all over – small ones can go in the paths as well so that winter and spring colour are assured. That way a pleasingly formal garden is achieved, but one which is capable of looking interesting for much of the year. For the formal minded, a knot garden consisting of nothing more than convoluted dwarf hedging in a geometric pattern with clean gravel in the interstices, can be decoratively pleasing, even if botanically limited.

EXISTING SITES

Inevitably not every garden you move to is situated on a new site. Sometimes, if you are lucky, you will inherit a plot from someone who has understood the problems of weather and has carried out the necessary defensive action against the wind. More often than not, you'll inherit a non-garden where the owner has made a desultory attempt to establish a lawn flanked by a few distorted shrubs. This does not prove that the place is impossible to turn into a garden – far from it. It just means they haven't been interested or been able to dis-

cover the potential.

Taking stock of the existing features has already been covered in length, but here are a couple of examples of the kinds of garden you might find on your hands.

Long, thin sites

Imagine a row of terraced houses. Their gardens are long and thin, the width of the house, perhaps running back a hundred feet or so. House No. 1 in the illustration is a typical rural mess with half the plot growing cabbages and the rest growing flowers for cutting – probably dahlias and chrysanthemums grown in rows. Their results are disappointing because the wind drives straight up the path, punished the cabbages and smashing through the chrysanthemum stems. Also, there's nowhere to sit outside. The best thing the occupants of Number 1 could do would be to look over their fence at the neighbours.

The garden in House No. 2 was laid out with more flair, but not much: a central path and a little lawn. The wind is stopped to a certain extent by a screen fence at the west end but still whistles over from No. 1. The woven birch fence erected by No. 3 helps to protect them from the south when the wind backs or veers.

All Rosa moyesii *hybrids have good hips. Here they contrast well with late perennials like sea holly and* Aster novae-angliae.

The little lawn is a nuisance to cut but does provide somewhere for the children to play in the summer.

House No. 3 have got their act together. They planted a hedge at the bottom of the garden and another a third of the way from the end – mainly to screen off the ugly vegetables but it helps cut the wind too. They decided that small lawns were more trouble than they were worth and bought some expensive stone flags to lay a patio which they then

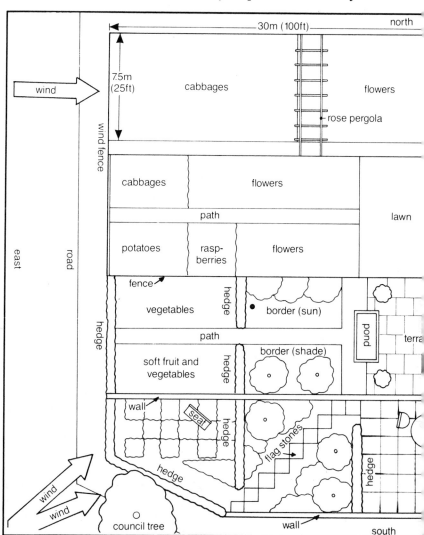

Fig. 7 Four gardens in a terrace or row of houses with varying degrees of shelter as described in the text.

bordered with a formal, rectangular pond.

West of this they kept the central path and laid out two small mixed borders with some fairly tall shrubs at the back on either side – an amelanchier, *Weigela florida*

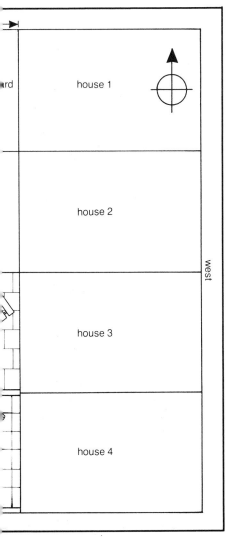

'Variegata' and a dwarf cherry on the south side (facing north) and a couple of repeat flowering shrub roses on the north side. In front are dwarf evergreen laurel *(Prunus laurocerasus* 'Otto Luyken') and the Mexican orange, *Choisya ternata.* These are all underplanted with low plants selected for colour.

House No. 4's occupants have joined several horticultural societies and have been keen gardeners for some years now. Their garden has been pinched off at the corner to make room for the public road but they don't mind because of the beautiful whitebeam the council planted on their boundary. It helps to protect their garden and makes a nice backdrop, just hiding the end of the tyre factory in the distance.

They had discovered buttress hedges and taken up bricklaying so it was a simple matter for them to build a 1.8 m (6 ft) wall along the south side of their territory. When the council compensated them for their corner they used the money to plant an expensive holly hedge at the end of their garden and to replace their vegetable plot with a little herb garden designed in a chequerboard scheme with antique stone flags separating the plants. The high

hedges make things a little dark in places, but they have grown a lovely collection of ferns and hostas, both of which thrive because the garden is now so sheltered. The buttress hedges run nearly the whole way across their narrow strip but slope sharply down to give the impression of a valley from the end. The path through the garden is staggered because of the position of the hedges, making it twice as long as their neighbours' and therefore making a stroll through the garden twice as interesting. Now

they are sheltered they can grow anything they like but when the hedges were developing they relied on sturdy perennials which needed no support. Red and pink potentillas, for example, blue catananche and the lovely pale yellow *Achillea* 'Moonshine' provided them with some summer colour. Dwarf tulips flower in the spring and hybrid musk roses, particularly the varieties 'Prosperity' (lemon to cream) and 'Penelope' (pale salmon) never failed to throw up a fragrant autumn finale. These were

Opposite: Anemone × hybrida *comes in pink shades or white. Perfect for late summer in dryish conditions.*

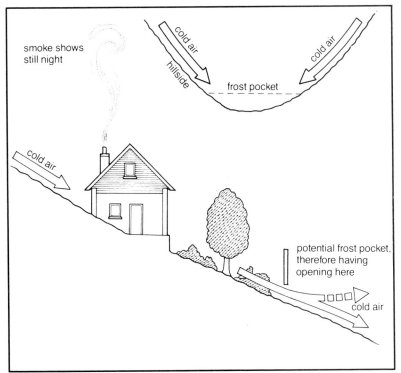

smoke shows still night

cold air

hillside

cold air

frost pocket

cold air

potential frost pocket, therefore having opening here

cold air

Left: Fig. 8. Frost pockets. Cold air is heavier than warm air and tends to slide down slopes, collecting in hollows. A hillside garden must have a downhill gap to allow cold air to escape.

supported by *Anemone hupehensis* which is so tough it will grow through concrete and stately blue spires of the late flowering monkshood *Aconitum × arendsii.*

Inevitably, as a result of everything growing up they have far more shade in the garden now and some of the sun-loving perennials have made way for lilies, hellebores, euphorbias and Himalayan poppies, but they still have plenty of sunny spots left for choice subjects like *Gentiana septemfida* and the Pacific Coast irises as well as somewhere to lounge about on sunbeds. Whether you inherit a new site or something as dispiriting as House No. 1 in this illustration, Garden 4 might well be something you should be aiming for. You may think it will take a decade to reach those standards, but even hedges mature surprisingly quickly, usually reaching their desired dimensions within four or five seasons.

Coastal problems
The problems of wind on the coast are compounded by salt spray and drifting sand, but at the same time coasts can be nearly frost free. Even as far north as Norway, the residual temperatures in the fjords are sometimes enough to allow

plants to survive which would not be hardy enough inland away from the sea. Looking around coastal resorts in Northern Europe, in Australia and in the Northern USA it seems that certain plants are favoured more or less to the exclusion of everything else. However, since many of these are highly decorative, it makes sense to stick to them for most of the planting and to be very cautious when trying out anything else. Hebes appear to be number one world favourites, followed closely by *Cordyline australis* or perhaps *Nerium oleander* in hotter areas.

The choice of good hedging material is wider in coastal regions where tamarisk, griselinia and pittosporum (in mild zones) can be added to the list. Tamarisk thrives in a maritime atmosphere and looks attractive throughout the summer. Its feathery foliage prevents it from being damaged too much by gales and the shrimp pink flowers are a worthwhile bonus. However, tamarisk makes poor clipping material, preferring to send a succession of arching branches up to a height of 2.4 m (8 ft) or more in good conditions. The New Zealand native *Griselinia littoralis* seems almost designed for hedging. Although a sharp frost will kill it, in coastal regions it cares not a toss for hurricanes or drenches of salt spray. The leathery foliage, unlike almost every other evergreen, is a pleasing, bright apple green changing to a tan colour on the stems. A thick griselinia hedge will help to keep wind out of the garden and reduces spray damage inside.

Occasionally, seaside gardens are themselves on very sandy soil which is liable to wind erosion. The secret here is to build up the body of the soil by adding organic matter and to ensure that as much of the surface is covered by growing plant material. Ground-cover plants help here and can be used to underplant shrubs such as elaeagnus, escallonia, viburnum and spiraea. Silver-foliage plants like santolinas, lavenders and most artemisias are happy in salty conditions and make attractive foils for roses. Roses are surprisingly salt tolerant. A thick plant cover helps to conserve soil moisture and prevent erosion.

FROSTY GARDENS

Most of this book is concerned with wind and its effects but one of the consequences of creating shelter is to increase the risk of frost. This is particularly so, not on hilltop sites, but where gardens are on the *side* of a hill. On still, clear nights, cold air rolls downwards and can get trapped in pools in lower parts of gardens. Sometimes, bark on the main stems of young trees and shrubs can split wide open as a result of such frosts. One solution is to make sure there is a good escape hole for the cold air. A gateway in the downhill hedge or fence, is often enough to let the cold air filter through.

Now that we have given some hypothetical examples, you should be developing some ideas of your own in relation to your garden. The rest of the book describes the enormous and fascinating range of plants that will survive harsh conditions. They are divided into sections covering all aspects of garden planning and each one is easy to grow and undemanding. However, once your plans have taken shape and your shelter plants are beginning to grow to a useful size, you will be able, later on, to choose whatever plants you fancy. But even if you stick to the plants listed in this book, preferring to keep to easy options, you will still be able to grow a beautiful, interesting and productive garden.

PLANTING THE BACKBONE

In any planting plan, especially when starting from scratch, selecting the right trees and shrubs is of fundamental importance. They become the garden's backbone and, on exposed sites, its armour as well. Putting mistakes right with trees is difficult and costly – both of time and money. They take a while to reach the necessary sizes to provide shelter and once the garden begins to grow up and fill out, removal of any shelter could make life uncomfortable for the rest of the plants.

We depend on the woody plants for much more than shelter from the elements. They provide good height in the garden, raising the focal points of borders and crowning the undergrowth with a decorative canopy. They also make attractive sight barriers, shutting one area off from another so that you are not obliged to view the entire garden in one sweeping glance. They help to get you through the dull months either with winter flowers, handsome twigs or long-lasting berries. There are conifers and evergreens to remind us there is still something alive out there, even in mid-winter, trees that have beautiful bark and eruptions of blossom in spring and then roses for continuity of colour. The smaller the space, the more discriminating we must be. The woody plants described below are divided into four groups: broad-leaved trees, shrubs, conifers and roses.

Opposite:
Euphorbias contribute to the spring border. E. epithymoides *is bright, early and fully hardy.* E. characias *(background) is subject to snow damage but quick to regenerate.*

Right: North American columbines make good early summer perennials, growing here with cranesbills.

TREES

Dimensions

L = Large = Ultimately higher than 10 m (30 ft)

M = Medium = Ultimately higher than 6 m (20 ft) (Less than 30 ft)

S = Small = Ultimately less than 6 m (20 ft)

ACER
maples

Small Japanese varieties are susceptible to weather but several large species are almost indestructible. All have good autumn colour. *A. pseudoplatanus* (sycamore) (L) and its cultivars are easy and quick to grow. *A. p.* 'Brilliantissimum' (M) has shrimp pink buds and golden-cream mature foliage. *A. p.* 'Scanlon' (S) stays neat for small gardens.

A. platanoides (Norway maple) (M) has equally fine cultivars. *A.p.* 'Crimson King' (M) has the darkest purple leaves of any in the genus. *A.p* 'Drummondii' (M) has well marked, variegated foliage, but an occasional inclination to revert to green.

A. saccharum. (Canadian sugar maple) (L) turns red in autumn, is fast growing and very hardy.

BETULA
birch

Tolerant of most conditions including thin, poor soil. Good autumn colour, lovely trunks and graceful habits. For screening, try *Betula pendula* (L) or *B. papyrifera* (L). Plant thickly, thinning after several years. Specimens: 'Youngii' (M) for graceful weeping habit; *B. utilis* (M) has coppery, peeling bark but *B. jacquemontii* (M) is dazzling white and has a fine trunk.

CARPINUS
hornbeam

Hardy deciduous trees, good for hedging, green leaves, hop-like fruits. *Carpinus betulus* (L) is best for hedges. American *C. caroliniana* (L) has good autumn colour.

CRATAEGUS
hawthorns

A rugged genus with many fine species. Suitable for hedging and screen planting as well as for specimen trees. Good blossom and fruit as well as pleasing shapes. *C. laciniata* (M) has lacy foliage and cream summer flowers. *C. oxyacantha* (M) has coloured cultivars including double red *C. oxyacantha* 'Paul's Scarlet' and pink *C. oxycantha* 'Rosea'. *C. prunifolia* (M) colours well in autumn and *C. tanacetifolia* (S) has grey, downy leaves with a good, twiggy winter outline.

FAGUS
beech

Fagus sylvatica and its cultivars are all weatherproof. Green and purple-leaved beech make fine hedges. *F. sylvatica* 'Dawyck' and 'Dawyck Purple' are fastigiate (erect) making useful specimens to use for restricted spaces. There are also weeping and golden forms. Look for *F. sylvatica* 'Rohanii' (L) a fern-leaved form with purple foliage.

FRAXINUS
ash
Fraxinus excelsior (L) (common ash) is too large for most gardens but excellent for big shelterbelts. There are also weeping forms.

ILEX
holly
Hollies can suffer in extreme cold and windy conditions but make good hedges. Varieties of *Ilex* × *altaclarensis* are fastest to grow. 'Golden King' (M) is a strong gold variegated form with berries. *I. aquifolium* 'J.C. van Tol' (M) is an excellent, nearly spineless, glossy green form. Coloured hollies can be used to highlight some of the more sombre evergreens.

LABURNUM
Medium or small tree which has lovely, hanging yellow blossoms in late spring. Good for thin soil. *L.* × *watereri* 'Vossii' (S) is nearly seedless (the fruits are poisonous) and has the longest racemes of flowers.

MALUS
apples
The tougher ornamental apples tolerate wind. Try *M.* 'Hillieri' (S) (bright pink flowers) and 'Golden Hornet' (S) whose yellow fruits persist through most of the winter. *M. profusion* is smattered with pink spring blossom.

POPULUS
poplars
Poplars are large, thirsty and invasive trees. They also ruin buildings if planted too near them, but, on the plus side, they make the quickest growing screen imaginable, and many are strikingly beautiful. *P.* × *candicans* 'Aurora' has pinkish-cream variegations and a pleasant balsam scent. *P. alba* has white, downy leaves and *P. tremula* 'quaking aspen' as its name would suggest, makes a sighing sound in the wind and appears to be all of a tremble. *P. lasiocarpa* has giant leaves.

PRUNUS
cherry, laurel, plum
P. lusitanica is described on page 33. *P. avium* (L) (wild cherry) in single and double forms, is windproof. For deep pink flowers and good autumn colour, plant *P. sargentii. (M)*

QUERCUS
oaks
Several oaks, especially *Quercus robur* (English oak) are weatherproof but too large for small gardens. *Q. frainetto* (L) is faster growing than most and *Q. ilex* (L) is evergreen. *Q.* × *tumeri* keeps its leaves until late winter.

SALIX
willows, see shrubs (page 68)

SORBUS
rowans and whitebeams

A valuable genus of decorative and weatherproof trees with good blossom, coloured berries and lovely foliage.

Whitebeams: *S. aria (L)* has downy, simple leaves. *S.a.* 'Lutescens' (M) is easiest to grow and has large foliage and good winter twigs but *S. a.* 'Chrysophylla' (S) has golden foliage turning deep yellow in fall.

Rowans: wild *S. aucuparia* (M) has red berries, Chinese *S. hupehensis* (M) has pink ones and *S.* 'Joseph Rock' (M) is deservedly popular for its amber fruits and rich bronze foliage in autumn. Look also for *S. aucuparia* 'Rossica' (M) for vigour and 'Winter Cheer' (S) for yellow berries.

TILIA
lime, linden

The small leaved lime, *Tilia cordata* (L), though seldom used as hedging material, thrives on heavy pruning and can make a thick screen or a network of 'pleached' limbs. Other species have graceful habits, particularly *T. petiolaris* (weeping silver lime) (L) which is a very good lawn tree, provided you have enough room. The scented flowers can make bees drunk!

Dimensions

L. Will reach 3m (10 ft)

M. Will reach 1.5m (5 ft)

S. Less than 1m (3¼ ft)

SHRUBS

AMELANCHIER
snowy mespilus

Attractive foliage and has abundant white blossom in mid-spring, plus some good autumn foliage on certain species. *A. canadensis* (L), is the toughest, forming thickets of suckers but *A. lamarckii* (M) has foliage tinted red when young, showing off the racemes of flowers and crimson leaves in autumn.

ARUNDINARIA
bamboos

Bamboos, in spite of their tropical appearance, are usually quite hardy. Their suckering habits make them useful for developing thick cover and most grow happily in either sun or shade. *Arundinaria anceps* (L), is one of the most vigorous, forming a thick, evergreen screen up to 6 m (18 ft) high. *A. japonica* (L) is a better known variety with larger leaves and deep green canes. For smaller sites, the foliage of *A. viridistriata* (S) is lime green striped with deep green – the colour is better in the sun. Shortest of all is the dwarf *A. pygmaea* (S), a good ground cover for harsh conditions that do not dry out too much.

AUCUBA
Japanese laurels
A useful group of hardy evergreens, many with well marked foliage. Several have golden variegations, either as broad splashes or small stipples. Though often planted in dense shade, the foliage colours better in half shade or full light conditions. *Aucuba japonica* 'Crotonifolia' (M) is mottle with gold flecks. *A. j.* 'Picturata' (M) is splurged with livid gashes of colour and needs careful siting. *A. japonica* 'Salicifolia' (M) deserves more favour, and its thin foliage goes well with clusters of scarlet berries.

BERBERIS
A huge genus of shrubs, mostly tough, often very thorny.
   Evergreens: *B. darwinii,* *(M)* is well known with massed yellow blooms in midspring and blackish-purple berries in autumn. *B. × stenophylla,* (L) flowers slightly later with large, arching branches. *B. julianae* (L) is a handsome evergreen with huge thorns.
   Deciduous: *Berberis thunbergii* (M) comes in several forms from the species which has bright red berries and green leaves to a dwarf hedging variety *(B. thunbergii* 'Atropurpurea Nana').

BUDDLEIA
Few species enjoy exposed gardens but *Buddleia davidii* and *B. alternifolia* are resilient, colourful and drought resistant. Look for *B. d.* 'Black Knight' (L) (dark purple), 'White Cloud' (L) and 'Royal Red' (L). Cut back annually to ensure stocky plants.

BUXUS
box
Good, evergreen hedging material. For dwarf hedges use *Buxus sempervirens* 'Suffruticosa' (S). Utterly hardy.

CAMELLIA
Not really suitable for growing in exposed gardens, but mentioned in the text for underplanting within shelterbelts.

CHAENOMELES
Japanese quince
Grown either as wall plants or free standing, Japanese quinces are unconcerned about harsh conditions and produce good winter blooms. *C. speciosa* (M) hybrids include 'Moerloosei' (white turning pale pink) and 'Nivalis' (pure white). The species is deep salmon and the cross *C. × superba* (M) has some outstanding cultivars including 'Crimson and Gold', whole blood-red petals contrast strongly with the golden stamens, and 'Pink Lady' which is a rich, strawberry pink.

CORDYLINE AUSTRALIS

This is an alien-looking affair of spiky leaves on gaunt stems (L). Good for mild, maritime areas where it braves the wind. Fragrant flowers bloom in early summer.

CORNUS
dogwoods

Alas, the really glamorous species need shelter, but there are several other striking shrubs. *Cornus mas* (M) – green and variegated forms available – has yellow midwinter flowers and little edible fruits (cornelian cherries). Various forms of *C. alba* have good foliage and colourful winter twigs: the gold form *C. alba* 'Aurea' goes well with darker *C. a. 'Kesselringii'* and in winter the red stems of the former look good with the black of the latter.

COTONEASTER

Another large genus of berry-bearing shrubs coming in all shapes and sizes.

Evergreen: *C. dammeri* (S) and *C. microphyllus* (S) run along the ground; both have deep red berries. *C. lacteus* (M) has relatively large leaves and is a late fruiter and good hedger. *C. conspicuus* (M) has beautiful summer blossoms as well as showy fruit.

Deciduous: there are many but *C. horizontalis* (M) makes excellent growth in spite of weather and it has very good berries too.

CYTISUS
brooms

Useful for thin, sandy soil, several have good green winter twigs. *C.* × *praecox* (M) makes clouds of cream blossom in spring. Colour forms of *C. scoparius* (M) (common European broom) are toughest. Look for 'Firefly' (yellow and bronze), 'Golden Sunlight' or *Cytisus* 'Windlesham Ruby' (mahogany crimson).

DEUTZIA

Deciduous shrubs which flower in early summer. Many dislike wind but *Deutzia* 'Mont Rose' is a vigorous grower with pale pink flowers in profusion.

ELAEAGNUS

Evergreen forms dislike deep frost but tolerate sea winds. *Elaeagnus* × *ebbingei* (M) (all green) and *E. pungens* 'Dicksonii' (M) (cream variegated) are the toughest varieties.

ESCALLONIA

Excellent for flowering coastal hedges. The shrubs have thick, deep evergreen foliage with abundant flowers. Irish bred 'Donard' varieties are excellent growers: 'Donard Pink' (M), 'Donard Beauty' (M) is red and 'Apple Blossom' (M) pink and white.

EUONYMUS

Resilient shrubs, with good fruits or fine evergreen foliage. *Euonymus europaeus* 'Red Cascade' (L) has wonderful red autumn foliage and pink fruits which crack open to reveal orange interiors. There are many evergreen forms: *E. fortunei* climbs—try growing 'Emerald and Gold' or 'Silver Queen'. *E. japonica* (L) makes a shiny evergreen bush and tolerates salt wind and industrial pollution.

GLEDITSIA

Gleditsia triacanthos (honey locust) (L). Ferny leaves, good autumn gold colour. Resists pollution and wind but can grow very large.

GRISELINIA

G. littoralis' covered on page 56. Excellent coastal hedging shrub.

HEBE

Not very frost hardy but certainly happy in coastal conditions. The smaller the leaf, the hardier they tend to be. In mild areas, try *Hebe* 'Autumn Glory' (S) (purple flowered evergreen) or 'Midsummer Beauty' (lavender). The dwarf *Hebe pinguifolia* is completely frost hardy.

HELICHRYSUM

Like most silver foliage plants, these are more susceptible to the wet than the frost. *H. splendidum* forms neat bushes with tiny silver leaves and little golden buttons. Prune hard in spring to keep it a compact shape.

HIPPOPHAE RHAMNOIDES
sea buckthorn

A natural coastal dweller with silvery foliage and orange berries persisting all winter (M).

HYPERICUM
St John's wort

Large genus with many garden-worthy species. *Hypericum calycinum* (rose of sharon) (S) is good, yellow-flowered ground cover. *H. patulum* 'Hidcote' (M) is more choice with huge, gold flowers.

KALMIA

Evergreens for acid soil. *Kalmia latifolia* (L) has sugar-pink flowers and glossy dark foliage.

KERRIA

One species, *Kerria japonica*, (M) is popular for its green stems, leaves and buttercup yellow flowers in spring. There is a double and a variegated form but purists prefer the natural species.

LAVANDULA
lavenders

All S. Aromatic. The silver foliage and lovely flower colour make these plants valuable for the exposed garden.

Neatest grower is *Lavandula angustifolia* 'Hidcote' (deep purple blue). Look also for 'Loddon Pink' and 'Munstead' (neat, blue). For more sprawling bushes try 'Old English'.

LIGUSTRUM
privet
Mostly hedge material (*Ligustrum ovalifolium* and cultivars) but some useful species too: *L. lucidum* (L) has glossy evergreen leaves and late summer flowers.

MAHONIA AQUIFOLIUM
Most mahonias need shelter but *M. aquifolium*, the Oregon grape (S), is evergreen, grows anywhere but is the poor relation of a good genus.

PARROTIA
Grown for its glorious autumn foliage, *Parrotia persica* (L) is good natured and can be trained or pleached as well as planted as a free-standing tree.

PHILADELPHUS
mock oranges
Useful shrubs which grow vigorously and have deliciously scented blossom in early summer. *Philadelphus* 'Beauclerk' (L) has purple centres to the flowers. 'Manteau d'Hermine' (M) is pure white and smaller in size. *P. coronarius* (M) has a good gold-leaved form which needs planting in partial shade to avoid any scorching. *P.* 'Virginal' (L) is one of the toughest varieties and has fully double blossoms.

PITTOSPORUM
Not hardy but suitable for mild coastal areas. *P. crassifolium* (L) is one of the best hedging species.

POTENTILLA
Tough little shrubs related to *Potentilla fruticosa* (S) and coming in various colour shades. Drought, frost and wind tolerant. Look for 'Elizabeth' (yellow), 'Day Dawn' (peachy pink), and the coppery 'Tangerine'.

RHODODENDRON
Huge and varied genus for acid soils. Toughest species is the purple-flowered *Rhododendron ponticum* (L) which is ugly and invasive. Small hybrids of *R. yakushimanum* (S) are resilient and good for restricted space. Rhododendron species and hybrids vary in hardiness and are always expensive to buy. It pays to consult a specialist and to make sure your soil is of a suitable type.

RHUS
sumach
Rhus typhina is a popular small tree with pinnate leaves and glorious autumn colour. Suckers, however, can be a problem.

Hellebores are indestructible and flower at the dullest time of year. This dark H. orientalis hybrid probably has some H. atrorubens in its breeding.

RIBES
flowering currants

Some fine shrubs, which are useful for screening. *Ribes sanguineum* (L) has pretty pink flowers in spring but unfortunately smells extremely unpleasant! *R. sanguineum* 'Brocklebankii' has golden foliage. *R. odoratum* (M) a suckering shrub has sweet scented yellow blooms in spring.

RUBUS
brambles

Several gorgeous species. *Rubus tridel* 'Benenden' (L) is smothered in large white blooms in early summer. *R. odoratus* (M) suckers freely, producing canes with huge, soft leaves. *R. cockburnianus* has showy canes for winter display.

SALIX
willows

A vast genus with species ranging in size from the miniscule *S. boydii* to the mighty *S. alba* which makes a vast windbreak. There are too many good species to list but all grow happily in exposed spots. Hedging and large shrub willows include *S. daphnoides* (L), *S. caprea (L)* and *S. pentandra (L)*. Weeping willow *(S. chrysocoma)* should be avoided. It is too big, too thirsty, but there are weeping forms of *S. purpurea* and *S. caprea* available.

Small willows include *S. hastata* with dark, glossy stems and white catkins, *S. arbuscula* which is ground hugging and *S. fargesii* (M) which has superb red winter twigs and broad leaves like magnolia.

SAMBUCUS
elders

Common black-berried elder has a dark-leaved form – *Sambucus nigra* 'Purpurea' (L) and the European red-berried species, a fern-leaved form – *S. racemosa* 'Plumosa Aurea' (L).

SANTOLINA
cotton lavender

Useful, mostly silver-leaved plants which are windproof if trimmed each year to keep them compact. The common *Santolina chamaecyparissus* has unattractive yellow buttons but *S. neapolitana* has cream flowers.

SENECIO
ragworts

One species, *S. greyi*, has good, grey foliage and bright yellow flowers. Must have dry conditions but doesn't mind wind or frost.

SKIMMIA

Good, low evergreens for acid soil. Fragrant flowers, red berries. Look for lily-of-the-valley scented *S. japonica* 'Fragrans' (S).

SORBARIA

Rampant, suckering shrubs which throw up huge screens of growth, regardless of wind. Creamy flowers in midsummer. *Sorbaria aitchisonii* (L) is the most vigorous.

SPIRAEA

White or pink flowered shrubs, not exciting but robust and easy. *S. × vanhouttei* has pure white sprays in early summer. *S. × bumalda* 'Anthony Waterer' produces pink clusters at the end of each stem.

SYMPHORICARPUS

snowberry

Excessively boring plants but they do grow into a thick mass of stems. The berries of *S. rivularis* are white and squashy – there are also pink forms such as 'Mother of Pearl'.

SYRINGA

lilacs

A rich genus of fragrant shrubs. Hybrids of *S. vulgaris* (L) are the toughest varieties. The one with the finest double white flowers is 'Madame Lemoine' and the strongest single red 'Charles Joly'. *Syringa × josiflexa* is an exciting alternative with huge flower panicles and soft colours. Look for *S. × j.* 'Bellicent' which has rose-pink flowers in summer and broadly ovate and pointed leaves.

TAMARIX

Tamarisk

This has been dicussed on page 56. Fine feathery shrubs for exposed, seaside sites. The most common and easiest to grow is *Tamarix gallica* (L).

ULEX

gorse

About the toughest plant going, but agony to handle because of its spines! It has handsome golden yellow flowers, and there is also a double form: *Ulex europaeus* 'Plenus' (M).

VIBURNUM

Another huge genus with many excellent shrubs.

Evergreen: *V. tinus* (M) makes a fine winter flowering hedge or screen. *V. tinus* 'Eve Price' has pink tinged flowers. *V. davidii* (S) has veined foliage and blue-black berries.

Deciduous: so many! *V. plicatum* has pure white summer flowers, *V. × bodnantense* is fragrant and flowers in mid-winter. *V. × carlcephalum* (L) is summer flowering, pink in bud opening, white and perfumed. *V. opulus* 'Xanthocarpum' is a yellow berried form of guelder rose.

WEIGELA

Vigorous shrubs flowering in early summer. *Weigela florida* is the easiest. Variegated and dark-leaved hybrids are easy to find and the flower colour ranges from 'Bristol Ruby' through pale pink to pure white 'Nivea'.

YUCCA

Though they may look tropical, yuccas are very tough. Most impressive, with 1.8m (6ft) flower spikes above the spiky leaves, is *Yucca gloriosa* (L). For smaller gardens, try the indestructible *Y. filamentosa* whose cream flowers reach a more manageable 90 cm (3 ft).

CONIFERS

Conifers can contribute a great deal to the planting plan, not only because most of them are evergreen but also because of their ability to withstand high winds and extremes of temperatures. There is a bewildering range of shapes, sizes and colours but only room to mention a few of the best species and cultivars.

ABIES

silver firs

There are several beautiful spieces in this genus whose needles are flattened and sometimes white underneath. One of the most popular is *A. koreana* (L) whose vivid green branches are graced with purplish cones from a fairly early age.

CEDRUS

cedars

Large trees with graceful silhouettes in maturity. *C. atlantica* grows well in harsh surroundings. There is also a blue form – *C.a. Glauca. C. deodar* has a more drooping habit.

CHAMAECYPARIS

false cypresses

A large group of trees with some invaluable members in a variety of shapes and shades, some good for hedging, others making more stately trees. *Chamaecyparis lawsoniana*, which has gold and blue-green forms, also features drooping, flattened branches. Try *C. l.* 'Ellwoodii' for stronger growth and *C. l.* 'Pembury Blue' is one of the best glaucous forms.

CRYPTOMERIA

Japanese cedar

Soft, lacy foliage changing with age. The old branches bend to the ground where they take root, developing a coppice effect. (L).

CUPRESSUS

cypress

Superficially similar to the false cypresses. *C. macrocarpa* is mentioned in the text as hedging material where frost is not too severe. It is also a good coastal plant.

Day lilies thrive in soil which does not dry out too much. New varieties are coming into cultivation every year but this 'Golden Chimes' has stood the test of time extremely well.

X CUPRESSOCYPARIS

The man-made hybrid of exceptional vigour, × *C. leylandii* was covered earlier. Should be planted with discretion. 'Castlewellan Gold', is a green-gold form.

GINKGO

maidenhair tree

Ginkgo biloba is a living fossil. It is deciduous, fully hardy with yellow autumn foliage.

JUNIPERUS

juniper

Genus of great garden value. Many colours and shapes from low, prostrate species like *J. conferta* and *J. horizontalis* 'Glauca' to tall, thin exclamation marks like *J. virginiana* 'Skyrocket' and *J. communis* 'Hibernica'.

PICEA

spruce

Shapely, often wind resistant and fast growing, spruces enjoy growing in groups. *Picea abies,* Christmas tree, can be clipped into a hedge. Most graceful of all is *P. brewerana* which has drooping limbs. *P. pungens* 'Koster' has blue-green needles.

PINUS

pine

A genus distinguished by its longer needles. Several are elegant: *P. coulteri* has extra long needles. *P. sylvestris* has orange-tan bark in mature trees but tends to be shallow rooted and can blow over in severe gales. The much shorter species, *P. mugo*, is capable of survival anywhere.

TAXUS

Yew has been discussed previously on pages 33 and 43. There are several garden forms of *Taxus baccata*. 'Irish' yew, *T.b.* 'Fastigiata' and its gold relative 'Fastigiata Aureomarginata' are useful for architectural planting but can splay badly after wet snow. Yew makes excellent hedges, should you be interested in formal clipped arrangements. As I said earlier in the book, good alternatives are hornbeam or beech.

THUJA

arbor-vitae

The usual colour-range of golds, blue-greens and greens, but different from the cypresses, and all have aromatic foliage. *T. occidentalis* has some fine cultivars: 'Rheingold' is a dwarf with amber leaves, 'Elegantissima' forms a sturdy golden pyramid.

TSUGA

hemlock

Two large trees in this genus: western hemlock, *Tsuga heterophylla* and eastern hemlock, *T. canadensis;* both come from parts of the world where winters tend to be excessively cold.

ROSES

No genus is quite so universal in gardens as *Rosa*. There are roses – either species or varieties – which will tolerate almost every kind of garden environment.

Most of the modern hybrids will grow happily in less than ideal surroundings but there are certain shrub roses listed below which are able to thrive in the most unfriendly conditions with minimal attention. They seldom need pruning and are also less prone to disease than others.

Rugosas

Because of their toughness and because they are so easy to grow, the wrinkle-leaf rose varieties deserve special consideration. They are perpetual flowering and most have attractive fruits.

'Agnes' Pale yellow, recurrent. Exquisite scent (L)
'Blanc Double de Coubert' White recurrent, scented. (L)
'Conrad F. Meyer' Pale pink, scented, recurrent (L)
'Kordes Robusta' Single scarlet, recurrent (L)
'Frau Dagmar Hastrup' Pale pink, single. Superb hips (M)
Rosa rugosa Cerise, recurrent single, hips (M)
'Roseraie de l'Haÿ' Wine purple, recurrent, scented, hips (M)
'Sarah van Fleet' Shell pink, recurrent, scented (L)

Other shrub roses

Hybrid Musks Repeat flowering shrubs, mostly vigorous and all scented. 'Buff Beauty' is apricot fading buff, 'Prosperity' lemon fading cream and, 'Penelope' salmon.

'Nevada' and **'Pink Nevada'** (also called 'Marguerite Hilling'). Strong shrubs covered in flower in midsummer and slightly recurrent.

***R. californica* 'Semi-plena'** Easy, vigorous shrub with deep pink flowers mid-season.

***R. rubiginosa.* Sweetbriar.** Apple-scented foliage, pink flowers. Several good cultivars including red 'Meg Merrilees'.

Ground-cover roses

'Nozomi' Glossy foliage, single white-tinged pink flowers.
'Max Graf' Large single pink flowers. Roots as it runs.
'Max Graf, Red' Similar but flowers red.
'Snow Carpet' Mats of double white flowers.
'Swany' Similar but more recurrent.

HERBACEOUS PLANTS

In the last chapter we listed a selection of trees and shrubs suitable for the skeleton or backbone planting of your garden. As well as taking the brunt of the winds, the tall woody plants will help to give your garden shape and form. They will be there in mid-winter as well as at the height of the growing season, providing architectural features with their outlines, dividing the garden up and providing attractive backgrounds for the rest of the plants. Without such a backbone, even a sheltered garden would appear very flat and boring but an exposed site would still be like Macbeth's 'blasted heath'!

At first, you'll want to go on making minor adjustments so don't worry if you are not quite sure whether you've got all the placings exactly right. Even the most gifted garden designers play a sort of 'musical plants' every autumn as they strive for perfect positioning and no one has yet got it right first time! As the trees and shrubs age the outline of your garden will change and mature but the overall layout will be

Opposite: *Some lungworts have spotted leaves, some plain green. On this cultivar,* Pulmonaria vallarsae *'Margery Fish', the spots have nearly merged. 'Argentea' has even more silvery leaves.*

Right: *In late summer, kniphofias and crocosmias provide plenty of colour but can be wiped out by sustained, severe frost unless grown on free-draining soil.*

taking shape and it is therefore time to begin thinking of fleshing it out with some herbaceous plants.

Many people, quite wrongly, underrate the importance of herbaceous plants. The dullness of gardens without them is proof enough of the enormous contribution they do make. They provide varied colour – often at times of year when it is badly needed. They may have bold or striking foliage which will stand out at a distance or which can grace the foot of a wall or be reflected in a pond. They make things change by growing quickly, flowering in their season and then dying away to make room for something else. While the shrubs and trees just get bigger, slowly but surely herbaceous plants can shoot up to a startling size, dazzle admirers with a brief display and then exit the stage. Finally, herbaceous plants are useful for filling up all those spaces and little areas of bare ground in between the woody plants. When you have also added some autumn and spring bulbs, and grown a climber or two through the shrubs themselves, you will have transformed your shrubbery into an interesting well-planted border.

Opportunities for interplanting with small plants will appear in some corners and disappear in others. Ringing the changes is easy with herbaceous plants because they mature and flower so quickly. Most look lovely within a season and often flower better when regularly disturbed. Very small perennials and alpines will be dealt with on pages 100-4 but here is a working list of easy herbaceous perennials, annuals and biennials which will enable you to add colour and tone to that work of art your garden is becoming.

PERENNIALS

Acanthus Large. Sun or half shade. Any soil, not too dry.
  Huge perennials with bold foliage and 90 cm (3 ft) flower spikes. Toughest is *A. spinosus* whose leaves are finely cut. Flowers (pink, green and white) appear from midsummer onwards.

Aconitum Medium to tall. Sun or partial shade. Any soil.

The monkshoods are tough with rigid stems that seldom blow over. Most are blue but *A.* × 'Ivorine' is cream and flowers in late spring. *A. napellus* – blue, or white and blue – flowers in midsummer growing to 1 m (3¼ ft). *A.* × *arendsii* is autumn flowering and reaches 1.5 m (5 ft) in rich, moist soil.

Achillea Medium. Full sun. Any soil.

Good-natured perennials for harsh conditions. Yellow varieties include *A. filipendulina* 'Coronation Gold', 90 cm (3 ft), and the elegant, silver leaved *A.* 'Moonshine', 45 cm (1½ ft). *A. millefolium* or yarrow has good coloured forms for the garden including 'Cerise Queen' which is strong wine pink. White varieties include *A. ptarmica* 'The Pearl' which enjoys damper soil and will reach 1 m (3¼ ft).

Anemone (Japanese) Tall. Sun or slight shade. Any soil.

A. × *hybrida* varieties are easy and tolerate poor soil, even growing up through paving. Late summer flowers are pink or white on 90 cm (3 ft) stems. Look for 'September Charm' and 'White Giant'.

Aquilegia Medium or small. Shade or sun. Any soil.

Columbines. Mostly blue or pink shades but American species brought reds and yellows into the hybrids. Easy from seed, lovely foliage and showy flowers in late spring. *A. alpina* is deep blue and the parent of many good hybrid strains. Best American hybrids are 'McKana' which come in red, mauve, cream and yellow, every flower having two colours.

Artemisia Medium or small. Sun. Dry soil.

Silver-foliaged plants revelling in the thinnest soils but hating wet. Cut back regularly to keep them young. *A. absinthium* 'Lambrook Silver' has the finest foliage. *A. ludoviciana* has white, felty foliage and creeping rootstock.

Aster Large and small. Sun. Any soil.

Traditional Michaelmas daisies are troublesome, needing staking and protection against mildew, but several rugged species exist: *A. amellus* needs no support at 45 cm (1½ ft). Varieties include 'Violet Queen' and 'King George' – deep blue in colour. *A.* × *frikartii* stays disease free. *A. novae-angliae* grows taller at 1.2 m (4 ft) and has good cultivars including the startling cerise 'Alma Pötschke' and a good white, 'Autumn Snow'. Twigs or pea sticks thrust into the ground around them will give adequate support and disappear as the foliage covers them.

Astilbe Medium or tall. Sun or shade. Moist soil.

Plume-like flowers in colours ranging from deep red through pinks to white. Good foliage. Height of some reaches 90 cm (3 ft) but hybrids like 'Fanal' (red) and 'Federsee' (pink) are shorter at 45 cm (1½ ft). Large hybrids include 'Ostrich Plume' (pink) and 'Deutschland' (white).

Astrantia Medium. Sun. Any soil not too dry.

Two species in cultivation: *A. maxima* has pink flowers, which look like little crowns, in midsummer and three-lobed leaves. *A. major* is more variable, usually white and green or pink and green, growing to 30 – 60 cm (1-2 ft). Seeds freely.

Campanula Various.

A huge genus. All species have bell-shaped flowers and most are easy to grow. Colours are usually blue or white or occasionally purple or mauve. *C. persicifolia* is easy, growing to 60 cm (2 ft) with showy blooms all summer. *C. carpatica* is shorter at 23 cm (9 in) with blue or white varieties. *C. lactiflora* grows tall at 1.2 m (4 ft) without needing much support.

Catananche Medium. Sun. Any soil.

One species, *C. caerulea*, grows masses of blue flowers with papery backs all summer. Grassy foliage.

Centaurea Medium or tall. Sun. Any soil.

Several rugged species. *C. montana* has deep blue flowers. Cut back to encourage further flowers. *C. dealbata* has cerise heads on 90 cm (3 ft) stems and *C. pulchra* 'Major' grows papery buds above fine, silver foliage.

Chrysanthemum Various. Sun. Good soil.

C. maximum (Shasta daisy) is one of the toughest perennials in cultivation. 'Wirral Supreme' is semi double and 'Phyllis Smith' has thin petals which look like shredded coconut.

Hybrid chrysanthemums such as Koreans tend to be short lived but are good to use for late colour. The pink button chrysanthemum, 'Mei-Kyo', is very perennial and old cottage hybrids like the single pink 'Sarah Curtis' are also worthwhile.

Convallaria Small, spreading. Shade. Any soil.

Lily-of-the-valley spreads well if happy and produces exquisitely scented white flowers in mid-spring. Slow to establish but hard to kill once planted.

Crambe Large. Sun. Any soil.

Crambe cordifolia has huge leaves and 2.4 m (8 ft) sprays

Foxgloves are sturdy British natives. Some people like the garden strain Digitalis purpurea *'Excelsior' shown here. Others prefer to stick to the wild form.*

of white flowers in early summer. *C. maritima* has blue-green, edible cabbagy leaves – useful foliage to contrast with darker specimens.

Dianthus Small. Sun. Limy soil.

Pinks are very hardy and don't mind wind. Their silver foliage is pretty and many varieties are strongly scented. Unnamed border seedlings provide plenty of colour. Look also for well-proven varieties like 'Doris', the laced 'Dad's Favourite' or the shaggy white double 'Mrs Sinkins'.

Sweet William, *Dianthus barbatus,* is a fine cottage plant which seeds itself and is excellent for cutting.

Epimedium Small. Shade. Leafy soil.

Really woodland plants, but some species are resilient and have attractive winter foliage. *E. pinnatum* is one of the toughest, with yellow spring flowers.

Erigeron Medium. Sun. Goodish, well-drained soil.

There are many hybrids of this daisy family member in shades ranging from white through mauves and pinks to deep blue. 'Darkest of All' is deep violet, and 'Förster's Liebling' is cerise.

One species, *E. aurantiacus,* has rich copper-orange flowers on 23 cm (9 m) stems in early summer.

Euphorbia Various. Shade or sun. Any soil.

A huge genus with many garden-worthy species. Flowers are usually greenish in colour, often coming out in winter or early spring. Creeping rootstocks occur on *E. robbiae,* 45 cm (1½ ft), evergreen, late winter flowering; and *E. griffithii,* 1.2 m (4 ft) which dies right back, has orange flowers and prefers damp soil. *E. characias,* 90 cm (3 ft), is shrub-like, loves sun and seeds freely.

Ferns Mostly shade. Some dry; some damp.

Too few ferns are grown. There are dozens of easy species which will multiply happily on their own. Those for dry(ish) shade which are easy, include *Phyllitis scolopendrium* (hart's tongue) with its garden forms. *Polypodium vulgare,* especially *P. vulgare* 'Cornubiense', and the soft shield fern, *Polystichum setiferum,* also cope with dry shade.

For moist conditions try *Matteuccia struthiopteris* (ostrich feather) and the lady fern, *Athyrium filix-femina.*

Geranium Various sizes. Some for dry soil, some damp.

(Not pelargoniums). Some of the cranesbills are remarkably tough. *Geranium pratense* grows up to 1 m (3¼ ft) or more in good soil and has blue flowers. *G. ibericum* is the showiest, with purple-blue flowers on 60 cm (2 ft) plants in full sun. There are garden forms of *G. sanguineum* (bloody cranesbill) including *G.s.* 'Album' (white) and 'Lancastriense' (pale pink). Look also for white *G. renardii* and aromatic *G. macrorrhizum* which makes a good groundcover and colours red in autumn.

Grasses

Many grasses and sedges grow well in exposed conditions. Tufty, blue-green *Festuca glauca* stays neat and small, *Avena candida* is a giant oat with flowers like fishing rods, and largest of all are the cortaderias or pampas grasses.

Sedges do not all need moisture. New Zealand native *Carex buchananii* has tan foliage and tolerates dry, windy conditions. *Carex stricta* has golden foliage and *C. pendula* is a woodlander with arching flower stems and deep green, bold foliage.

Watch for invasive pests like *Phalaris arundinacea* 'Picta' or gardener's garters, planting them judiciously.

Helenium Tall. Full sun, medium soil.

A useful genus for late summer flowers in autumn colours – golden, russet or brown. The shorter varieties are less likely to blow over in the wind. Try 'Crimson Beauty', 'Wynd-ley' (orange yellow) or *H. pumilum*. Tall varieties need staking but are superb cut flowers. Look for 'Bruno' (brown-red) and 'Butterpat'.

Hellebore Medium. Sun or shade. Any soil.

Every species is gardenworthy. Most flower in winter or spring and vary in colour from dark purple-rose *(H. atrorubens)* through various shades of green *(H. corsicus, H. foetidus)* to purest white *(H. niger.)* Seek them out and then treasure them!

Hémerocallis Large. Sun or partial shade. Not too dry.

Tough and rugged, day lilies will establish themselves in poor conditions as long as they are not too dry. Massive clumps form which can be divided every few years to maximize flowering. Unfortunately, there are some vile pink hybrids about these days but the orange, tan and yellow shades are all worth seeking out. Try 'Corky' (sharp yellow) or larger flowered 'Lemon Bells'. 'Bright Spangles' is vibrant orange and 'Berlin Red' deep maroon.

Hosta Medium. Shade. Moist soil.

Provided the soil is not too dry, hostas will tolerate a surprising amount of wind and spread to form a good, solid ground cover. *H. sieboldiana* has the largest, glaucous leaves, but *H. fortunei* has the best range of leaf colours. Look for new golden varieties like 'Gold Standard' and for variegated forms like 'Thomas Hogg' that keep their colour all summer.

Iris Medium or tall. Some wet, some dry. Sun. Any soil.

Tall bearded iris hybrids get knocked down in wind but dwarf and intermediate strains like 'The Bride' and 'Langport Wren' (deep garnet) stand up well. *Iris sibirica* likes moist soil but is an indestructible plant. *I. foetidissima* grows in dry shade and has pretty orange fruits in winter. *I. pallida* 'Variegata' has silver-striped leaves.

Kniphofia Large, medium and small. Free-draining soil. Sun.

Sometimes susceptible to severe frosts, but the red hot pokers are unmoved by wind. There are several fine colour forms and one or two charming species. *Kniphofia galpinii* comes out in late summer with tangerine flowers, 45 cm (1½ ft). *K.* 'Early Buttercup' has strong yellow flowers in late spring and deep green foliage. Pale greenish-white 'Little Maid' and the caramel-tipped 'Toffee Nosed' are recent hybrids of great beauty.

Lamium Small. Anywhere. Any soil.

Weed-like in their invasive habits, forms of *Lamium maculatum* are nevertheless useful garden plants. The striped-leaf kinds come in several shades of pink, but queen of them all is 'White Nancy' whose leaves are uniform silver and whose flowers are white. There is a gold-leaved deadnettle but its purple pink flowers look unattractive against the jaundiced foliage.

Lychnis Small or medium. Sun. Any soil.

Good-natured plants with pink or red flowers which highlight mixed borders well. *L. flos-jovis* has silver foliage with short stems, 20 cm (8 in), of sugar-pink flowers. *L. coronaria* is also silver leaved with 60 cm (2 ft) high wine-red flowers, surpassed only by the white form, *L. coronaria* 'Alba'. *L. chalcedonica* reaches 1 m (3¼ ft) and has blood-red flowers, which are shaped like the cross of St. John – they will need staking.

Melissa Medium. Sun or partial shade. Any soil.

Not the most beautiful of plants but the creeping rootstock ensures a good, solid ground cover and the foliage smells of lemon when bruised. Look for the golden variegated form and the gold-leaf form.

Nepeta Medium. Sun or slight shade. Any soil.

Common catmint. Easy to

grow, drought and wind tolerant. The hybrid *Nepeta* 'Six Hills Giant' is taller and coarser. A good plant for lining the hedge bottom as long as it doesn't have wet feet in winter!

Papaver Large or medium. Sun. Rich soil.

Though easily wind-bashed, with a little support the big oriental poppies make a stunning early summer display. The strongest hybrid is 'Goliath' – an unbelievable bright red – but modern, dwarfer stains like 'Oriana' or 'Redizelle' cope with poor weather more effectively.

Polemonium. Small or medium. Sun. Any soil.

Jacob's ladders. Some, like *P. caeruleum*, are invasive, seeding everywhere. Others, like *P. foliosissimum*, are more restrained. Most have blue or white flowers but those of *P. carneum* are shell pink and, crossing with blue species throws some delightful purple and mauve offspring. Of these, *P.* 'Lambrook Mauve' is a charming dwarf easily propagated by splitting in spring.

Potentilla. Medium. Sun. Goodish soil.

People mistake them for strawberries or geums – they're in fact related to both. The pink and red species are finest for most plantings. 'Gib-

son's Scarlet' is brighter than the blood red *P. atrosanguinea* which has silvery, strawberry foliage. Best of the pinks is *P. nepalensis* 'Miss Willmott'. Yellow and orange species include *P. recta* and *P. tonguei*.

Polygonum Various. Some sun, some shade. Various soils.

Robust relatives of the dock. For tall species try *P. amplexicaule* or *P. bistorta* 'Superbum'. Spreading ground-cover species include *P. affine*, of which the best is 'Donald Lowndes', and *P. vacciniifolium*.

Pulmonaria. Small. Shade or partial shade. Any soil.

The lungworts. Lovely pink, blue or white flowers in spring. Broad foliage, stippled or blotched with silver. Look for *Pulmonaria saccharata* (spotty, with blue and pink flowers) and *P. rubra* (non-spotty leaves with clear pink flowers). Though happier in the shade, they will also tolerate some dryness but tend to get mildew if too dry.

Ranunculus Various. Sun. Any soil.

Several buttercups make good garden plants. *R. gouanii* has large yellow flowers in early spring, 23 cm (9 in) and later, the double form of *R. acris*, the field buttercup, is covered with yellow buttons, 60 cm (2 ft). *R. gra-*

mineus is a beautiful species with grass-like foliage and glossy yellow flowers. *R. aconitifolius* 'Plenus' (fair maids of Kent/France) has pretty white buttons and deep green foliage.

Salvia Medium. Sun. Dryish soil

A huge genus, most species of which are only suitable for sheltered gardens, but those of northern origin such as *S.* × *superba* are very hardy. The best hybrids come from Germany and include 'Lubeca', 'May Night' and 'East Friesland'. They are various shades of blue with deep calyces.

Scabiosa Medium. Sun. Not too dry.

The cutting flower *Scabiosa caucasica* is a fine border plant and, although it comes in several shades, the old variety 'Clive Greaves' is still the most popular. There is a good white, 'Mount Cook'. *Knautia macedonica* is a close relative with 60 cm (2 ft) stems and deep port-wine red flowers.

Sedum Medium. Sun. Any well-drained soil.

Most sedums belong in the alpine section but cultivars of *S. spectabile* are superb plants for exposed gardens. They flower in the late summer, are beloved by butterflies and have attractive dead heads for winter. Better than the species is the cultivar 'Autumn Joy' whose flowers last deep into autumn. Late butterflies love 'Autumn Joy' just as much as the pure species.

Stachys Medium. Sun. Good soil.

The felty leaved *Stachys lanata* (lamb's ears) is a fine foliage plant, often used on border edges. *Stachys spicata* and betony *(Stachys officinalis)* have purple or lavender flowers and handsome foliage.

Symphytum Medium or large. Shade. Any soil not too dry.

Small comfreys such as *Symphytum grandiflorum* make good, if rather coarse ground-cover plants. The taller comfreys get blown down in the wind but they will regenerate readily from massive taproots.

Tradescantia Medium. Shade or sun. Any good soil.

A North American native, subject of considerable breeding but even the modern hybrids are a bit too leafy, although they have triple-petalled blooms of great charm. 'Isis' is deep blue, 'Osprey' white with blue overtones and 'Purewell Giant' a rather startling purple.

Trollius. Medium or tall. Shade or sun. Moist soil.

The globe flowers are surprisingly tough and quite prolific if happy. *T. europaeus* hybrids include 'Goldquelle', a clear yellow, and 'Superbus', a cool greenish-yellow colour. *T. ledebourii* 'Golden Queen' has curious petaloid stamens emerging from the flower centres as orange tufts.

Verbascum Tall. Sun. Any soil not wet.

Some mulleins are too tall for exposed gardens but *V. blattaria* 'Alba' can handle any weather and has lovely beige and white flowers with purple centres. *Verbascum phoenicium*, though it may reach 1.2 m (4 ft), is usually strong enough to stand in all but the worst winds.

Veronica. Medium. Sun. Any soil.

Speedwells can be splendid garden plants. *Veronica gentianoides* forms neat cushions of foliage with spires of palest blue flowers in early summer. There is also a fine variegated form. *V. spicata* has attractive foliage and blue, lavender or pink spikes.

ANNUALS

Although they can only reproduce themselves from seed, annuals and biennials do not always need resowing. They frequently develop regenerative colonies on their own in your mixed borders. Annuals can be introduced to fill gaps with quick colour and to grow in places where other species seem unable to get established – either because it is too dry or too exposed. Here is a short list of useful annuals and biennials:

Calendula Pot marigold. Orange and yellow rays. Easy, flowers nearly all year. Grows to 30 cm (1 ft).

Campanula Canterbury bell. Bold cups in early summer. Buy plants or sow in rows and then transplant.

Centaurea cyanus Cornflower. The blue species is better than the coloured hybrids. Sow in autumn for bushy plants. Loves the sun. Grows to 60 cm (2 ft).

Clarkia Unobtrusive but pretty annuals in a good colour range. Sow spring or autumn and thin to 20 cm (9 in) apart.

Dahlia Often grown as annuals, bedding dahlias can be useful for filling gaps. Buy plants ready grown or sow seed under glass in the late winter. Try the 'Redskin' strain which has good foliage.

Delphinium Larkspur – another lovely cornfield weed.

The wild species is peacock blue. Pink and white forms are available for gardens. Grows to 60-90 cm (2-3 ft).

Digitalis Foxgloves. Biennials of great character, sowing themselves happily in the shade. Select your own pale strains by weeding out dark-stemmed seedlings, or alternatively let nature take her course.

Eschscholzia Californian poppies self seed happily in dry sunny conditions. Mainly orange and yellow but there are cream, pink and salmon shades too. Glaucous, ferny foliage. Grows to 30 cm (1 ft).

Glaucium Horned poppy. *G. phoenicium* has blue foliage and bright orange flowers. Grows to 60 cm (2 ft).

Hesperis Sweet rocket. Biennial, scented mauve or white flowers. Grows to 90 cm (3 ft).

Iberis Candytuft. Rapid annual – perfect for filling gaps. Pretty pink or white flowers, short lived.

Impatiens Universally popular bedding plant. Handy because of the huge range of colours and many grow and flower well in the shade. Not windproof but wind damage repairs itself by quick growth.

Annuals like these Californian poppies, Eschscholzia, *make self-perpetuating colonies in sunny conditions. They are bone hardy.*

Hesperis matronalis, *Dame's violet or sweet rocket is an easy biennial with soft colours and evening scent. It prefers moisture.*

Lathyrus Sweet peas. In exposed gardens go for dwarf varieties that will not get blown off their supports. Try 'Bijou' or 'Cupid'.

Limnanthes *L. douglasii* is a low annual covered with yellow and white flowers in early summer. Invasive but a stunning carpeter. Grows to 15 cm (6 in).

Lunaria Honesty. Fine biennial with magenta or white flowers and pretty, flat seed pods. Look for perennial species *L. rediviva*. Grows to 60 cm (2 ft).

Myosotis Forget-me-nots will multiply themselves in the right conditions and make lovely backgrounds for spring bulbs. They come in pink and white but traditional blue is the best.

Nicotiana Tobaccos, though half hardy, tolerate windy gardens and smell so good at night – sometimes the only calm part of the day! Grows to 90 cm (3 ft).

Nigella Love in a mist. Another self-perpetuating annual. Blue with lacy foliage. Grows to 45 cm (1½ ft).

Papaver Shirley poppies are improved cornfield weeds. Pink, salmon, lemon and white shades turn up, as do reds. Grows to 45 cm (1½ ft).

Petunia Half hardy but surprisingly wind tolerant – it's the rain they hate. Grows to 30 cm (1 ft).

Rudbeckia Wonderful marmalade-coloured daisies for filling autumn gaps. Grows to 90 cm (3 ft).

VERTICAL GARDENING

Exposed gardens with screens or artificial wind barriers provide a worthwhile opportunity for vertical gardening. Too often we view our plots in two dimensions forgetting that, in a small garden particularly, a significant proportion of the surface area where plants can grow and thrive may be vertical rather than horizontal. A rectangular plot, for instance, measuring 10 by 20 m (33 by 66 ft) provides a ground area of 200 m² (240 sq yd). Surround this with a fence or wall, 2 m (6½ ft) high and you have another 120 m² (144 sq yd) to furnish – more than half the ground area. So it does pay to give a good deal of thought to the vertical aspects of your garden.

As soon as a wall or fence is erected, there will be a change in the environment on either side. If it runs from east to west, the south side will be warm and bright, facing the sun most of the day. (The reverse is true in the Southern Hemisphere.) East-facing walls get early sun but tend to be cold. A southwest aspect provides the gentlest conditions unless the prevailing winds come from that direction. Even then, frost and cold are less likely to do damage there than elsewhere.

The plants listed below will grow well, even in exposed conditions. Some will put up with a cold, north wall and are marked as such in the text. Others, though less suited to such conditions, will tolerate more moderate shade. After each name, planting aspects (north/east and so on) are suggested in order of the plant's preferences.

WOODY AND HERBACEOUS CLIMBERS

Actinidia Deciduous. S/W/SE. Vigorous. Any soil. *A. chinensis* (kiwi fruit) will not produce a crop in exposed gardens, but has handsome, hairy stems, large leaves and covers wide areas quickly.

A. kolomikta is a less rampant type, having leaves splashed with white and pink blotches.

Camellia. Evergreen. SW/W/N. Needs acid or neutral soil. Though they need shelter to flower well, camellias will succeed on a wall, even in chilly gardens. Go for hardy, late flowering hybrids of *C. japonica* like 'Virgin's Blush' (white flushed pink) 'Lady Clare' (peach-pink) or 'Kimberley' (red).

Chaenomeles Deciduous. E/ NE. Any soil.
Superb wall plants creating a good area for other climbers. (see page 63).

Cotoneaster (see page 64)

Clematis
An invaluable genus with species suitable for almost every situation. The familiar, large-flowered hybrids dislike wind which damages their young growths, but there are plenty of superb varieties which will tolerate poor conditions. All clematis are lime tolerant and like soil which does not dry out too much.

Montana types Deciduous. N/S/E/W. Any soil.
All flower in late spring when the plants are then completely smothered in bloom. *C. montana* has small white flowers but *C. chrysocoma sericea* is similar in every respect except the flowers which are purer white and larger. Look for *C. montana* 'Tetrarose' (deep pink) and *C. montana* 'Wilsonii' which flowers a month later than the others.

Orientalis types Deciduous. N/S/E/W. Any soil
The yellow-flowered clematis which bloom in late summer and autumn. All have showy seedheads, lasting well into the winter months. *C. orientalis* has rounded flowers with thick sepals like orange peel; *C. serratifolia* has lemon-scented flowers which are the colour of parchment.

Viticella types Deciduous. N/S/E/W. Any soil.
Small-flowered hybrids in jewel-like colours. Cut back to ground level every spring to ensure new, vigorous growth. Perfect for growing through other climbers or shrubs. *C. viticella* is blue, 'Minuet' is purple with a white centre, 'Rubra' is red, 'Alba Luxurians' white with green tips and 'Royal Velours' a rich purple colour. *C. viticella* 'Etoile Violette' has larger flowers of deep violet-blue which look good among golden foliage.

Other clematis *C.* × *jackmanii* (deep blue) and *C.* × *j.* 'Superba' (purple) are the easiest to grow of the large-flowered hybrids, shooting up from the roots quickly, even when cut back by frost. The red 'Ville de Lyon' is wind-proof but an unattractive flat red. 'Mrs Cholmondeley' is pale lavender blue and vigorous, flowering well into autumn.

Eccremocarpus scaber Herbaceous climber. S/SW/W. Any soil.
The glory vine, producing successions of orange-red flowers all summer. Easy to grow from seed but is usually killed off each winter.

Forsythia suspensa Deciduous wall plant. W/E/N. Any soil.
It is smothered with yellow flowers in spring, is dull at other times, but supports clematis and other climbers. Enjoys facing north but flowers more freely in full light.

Garrya elliptica Evergreen wall plant. E/N. Any soil.
Dark evergreen with lustrous foliage and long winter catkins on male plants. Good for supporting and protecting other climbers.

Humulus Herbaceous climbers. W/E/N. Any soil.
The golden hop, *H. lupulus* 'Aureus', is the finest form with leaves which contrast well against a dark background. The common hop is a vigorous climber. Select females for their attractive green flowers.

Hydrangea petiolaris Deciduous climber. E/N/W. Any moist soil.
It is happy in deep shade, but flowers better in partial shade. Lovely spring foliage, contrasting with the tan stems; creamy, lace-cap flowers in summer. Clings by adventitious roots.

Jasminum Evergreen or deciduous climbers. E/N/W/S. Any soil.
Summer jasmine, *J. officinale*, has fragrant white flowers and needs the protection of a wall in cold areas. *Jasminum nudiflorum* loses its leaves, but has deep green stems and the bright yellow winter flowers stand out against them.

Lathyrus Herbaceous climbers. W/S/E. Any soil not acid.
The perennial peas are valuable for summer colour. Easiest to grow is *L. latifolius*, the 'everlasting', usually purple-pink in colour but has white forms and pale intermediates. Tolerates drought conditions, flowering profusely in full light. Try the Persian native *L. rotundifolius* which has brick pink flowers for most of the summer.

Lonicera Honeysuckle. Any moist soil, roots in shade E/W. Another important genus with many hardy species, often scented.

L. periclymenum and cultivars are scented and flower in partial shade. E/W Keep the roots cool and moist by regular mulching. Earliest flowering is 'Belgica' or early dutch, which blooms profusely in the spring. 'Serotina' flowers over a longer period from midsummer. Both have reddish petals with cream throats.

L. japonica has cream flowers, superb scent and is almost evergreen in mild areas. Improved types include 'Aureoreticulata' (gold-netted foliage) and 'Halliana' which is more hardy than most.

L. × *brownii* hybrids have scentless, red flowers which do not curve like other species. 'Dropmore Scarlet' is the easiest of these to grow and flowers continuously after midsummer.

L. × *tellmanniana* is also scentless but the vivid orange-yellow flowers, flecked with scarlet, make it a colourful early summer climber.

Polygonum baldschuanicm
Deciduous climber. N/S/E/W. Any soil.
To many, this is a repulsive weed, smothering everything in its path as it rampages its way through the garden. It will, however, grow anywhere and covers ugly objects. It has white flowers from mid to late summer.

Parthenocissus Deciduous climbers. W/E/N. Any soil.
The popular Virginia creeper, *P. quinquefolia*, has several

Climbing plants look well if allowed to grow into each other. Here, honeysuckle and Clematis montana intertwine.

useful relatives all of which colour well in autumn and grow vigorously on exposed walls. *P. tricuspidata* is often confused with Virginia creeper, but has simple or three-lobed leaves.

Pyracantha Deciduous wall plants. W/E/S. Any soil.
Firethorns are not always reliably hardy in frosty areas but are quick-growing plants with good berries. *P. coccinea* is the most common with red or orange berries but look for *P.* 'Watereri' which has larger orange berries.

Vitis – vines Deciduous climbers. S/W/E. Any soil.
Grape vines are surprisingly hardy and have lovely foliage which looks fresh all summer. *Vitis vinifera* 'Purpurea' is a dark-leaved grape with good autumn colour. *Vitis coignetiae* can climb to the top of the highest trees. Its huge leaves turn the colour of old claret in autumn.

Wisteria Deciduous climbers. S/W. Any soil.
Wisterias are perfectly hardy but will only flower if the wood is ripened by a good, hot summer. Therefore, in cold areas a hot wall is essential to achieve good displays of blossom. There are many cultivars, most of which take up to a decade to flower reliably but *W. sinensis* is an early starter.

ROSES

Here is included a tiny selection of the many reliable roses available to gardeners on exposed sites.

Species

R. filipes A rampaging rose growing to 10 m (30 ft) or more. Flowers small, white and single, produced in profusion in early summer. Non-recurrent.

R. longicuspis Nearly evergreen in mild areas. A vigorous rambler with cream, banana-scented flowers in mid summer and good, red hips. Non-recurrent, grows to 5 m (18½ ft). *R. longicuspis* is excellent up a tree.

R. moschata The musk rose. Has single cream flowers, scented of musk. Vicious, hooked thorns. Grows to 3 m (10 ft) – another one to scramble up a tree.

Ramblers

'Albertine' Non-recurring, salmon pink, double flowers with faint fragrance. Good foliage and dark stems, a tough survivor flowering in mid-summer.

'Alberic Barbier' Dark, glossy foliage, vigorous growth and faintly scented, ivory-white flowers in mid-summer. Slightly recurrent. Would tolerate north wall.

'Félicité et Perpétue' Very vigorous, grows to 6 m (20ft). Has clusters of fragrant, double flesh-coloured buds, opening soft white.

'Goldfinch' Nearly thornless, vigorous rambler which grows up to 4 m (13 ft) with apricot buds opening to semi-double cream flowers. Strongly fragrant flowers.

'Veilchenblau' To some a curiosity rather than a thing of beauty. Identical in shape and habit to 'Goldfinch', but the flowers are a liverish-purple with startling yellow stamens.

'Wedding Day' A rampant rambler which grows 8 m (26 ft) with a mass of non-recurrent single flowers in mid-summer. They open as a pale yellow colour and fade to cream.

Climbers

'Altissimo' Has a good single red flower which repeats a little. Hips are produced, but if you want repeat flowers you must first dead-head the plant. A good alternative is 'Scarlet fire' ('Scharlachglut').

'Danse du Feu' Has bright scarlet, recurrent, double flowers with faint scent. One of the easiest red climbers to grow.

'Gloire de Dijon' This is a unique buff-apricot colour with very full, quartered flowers and strong fragrance. Recurrent and though susceptible to mildew, this plant is, in fact very hardy.

'Golden Showers' Not very tall but has good foliage and a constant supply of strong yellow buds opening to flowers which fade to a primrose colour and look good until the petals fall.

'Lady Waterlow' Vigorous, recurrent climber with well-shaped, strongly-scented, salmon-pink flowers and healthy foliage.

'New Dawn' One of the finest and toughest climbers with superb vigour, glossy green foliage, pale pink well-formed flowers with a slight fragrance, and recurrent.

BULBS

The quickest way to create a colourful garden display is to plant masses of bulbs. They are not always cheap to buy, but most are easy to grow, are tolerant of poor conditions and provide lots of colour without taking up much space. Even daffodils, whose aftermath looks so untidy, can be grown so that the withering foliage is disguised by other plants which follow on. Alternatively, they can be integrated painlessly into a natural grass and wildflower sward.

When buying and planting, it is important to abide by a few basic rules. Always buy bulbs from reputable suppliers, selecting good, firm ones and planting them as soon as possible after purchase. Bulbs bought by post should be examined carefully on arrival and planted without delay. Plant deeply enough to ensure that the layer of soil above the bulb is at least as thick as the bulb – eg an 8 cm (3 in) bulb must be at least 8 cm (3 in) deep. After a few years, it may be necessary to lift and divide congested clumps, re-planting the bulbs singly. I prefer never

Left: *Much winter colour comes from bulbs and corms. In January, aconites* Eranthis hyemale, *soon to be followed by* Cyclamen coum.

Opposite: *Colour is a matter of personal preference. Here the brilliance of the climbing rose* 'Danse du Feu' *is lost among other climbers and colourful annuals.*

to cut foliage back but always to allow it to dry up and disappear of its own accord, even if this takes until mid-sumer.

Although the majority of bulbs flower in early spring, at a time when cheerful colour is most badly needed, there are plenty of species which are at their best in the other seasons. Here is a good and varied selection of bulbs for year-round colour and interest in your garden.

WINTER

Crocus

Several species flower in later winter. Easiest to grow is *C. tomasinianus* (lilac mauve). Look for the darker 'Whitewell Purple'. *C. ancyrensis* 'Golden Bunch' is the colour of egg yolk and there is a range of shapely *C. chrysanthus* varieties – 'Snow Bunting' (cream and lilac stripes), 'Zwanenburg Bronze' (orange and purple-bronze) and 'E.A. Bowles' (butter-yellow).

Cyclamen

Cyclamen coum flowers throughout frost and snow. The carmine blooms are set off by decorative foliage. Grows to 10 cm (4 in).

Eranthis

Winter aconites. Little gold blossoms, each set in a green ruff. Spreads by seeding and looks attractive with snowdrops.

Galanthus

Many species of snowdrop are available, providing flowers at different stages of the winter. *Galanthus nivalis* is the most common but try *G. elwesii* for its larger flowers and improved named cultivars, like 'Straffan' and *G. nivalis* 'Sam Arnott', both of which are twice the size of common snowdrops.

SPRING

Anemone

A large genus with some rugged species. *Anemone x fulgens* is a rich scarlet colour and flourishes in the sun. *A. blanda* tolerates sun or shade, flowering in mid-spring (blue). Good cultivars include 'White Spendour' and 'Radar' (pink). Florists' anemones provide lovely cut flowers.

Fritillaria

Fritillaria imperialis (crown imperial) can grow 15 cm (6 in) a day in mid-spring and, though tall at 90 cm (3 ft) can handle rough weather. Smaller species are equally tough and may of them are drought resistant. *F. pyrenaica* is much shorter at 20 cm (8 m) with purple-brown bells.

Muscari

Grape hyacinths may be commonplace but will grow lustily wherever they are planted and will always multiply well. *Muscari armeniacum* has some tough cultivars like 'Blue Spike' but *M. botryoides* is less coarse. There is also a charming white form – *M. botryoides* 'Alba'.

Narcissus

Daffodils and narcissi are so universal that they barely need a mention here except to point out that they are common because they are such delightful and easy garden subjects. Shorter varieties with smaller flowers tend to be less prone to wind damage. When choosing bulbs don't forget to spread the season by selecting early and late bloomers. *Early:* 'Peeping Tom' – an elegant daffodil with reflexed petals. *Mid:* 'King Alfred' – a common yellow daffodil that has stood the test of time. *Late:* 'Pheasant Eye' *(N. poeticus recurvus),* white with a red eye.

Tulipa

Nearly as common as the daffodils but never as good at multiplying themselves. Short and early varieties seem the most weather-proof but *T. fosteriana* 'White Emperor' is worth mentioning because, although it is tall with huge flowers, it can withstand a fair buffeting from the wind. Dwarf hybrids, particularly doubles, last well and some of the species tulips thrive on privation. Of these, *T. greigii* 'Red Ridinghood' has chocolate-striped folige with red flowers and *T. kaufmanniana* 'Heart's Delight' is red on the outside opening to a pale-rose pink. Both reach 25 cm (10 in).

Scilla

Also, the allied *Chionodoxa, Puschkinia* and *Hyacinthus.* These are small and middle-sized, mostly blue or white flowered spring plants which love colonizing gravel or spreading about under trees. Deepest blue scilla is *S. sibirica* 'Spring Beauty'.

SUMMER

Allium

There are many decorative onions. Chives *(Allium schoenoprasum)* has pretty mauve flowers, *A. karataviense* has striking purple foliage and *A. albopilosum* has huge, globe-shaped seed heads. Tall members include *A. siculum* with its distinctive nodding flowers, whose stems become erect after fertilization, and *A. giganteum* which has purple globes at 1.2 m (4 ft). *A. moly* has bright yellow flowers in spring.

Crocosmia

These are showy perennials growing from corms. Many are tender but *C. masonorum* is easy, if a little invasive. The orange flowers appear in late summer.

Galtonia

Galtonia candicans (summer hyacinth) flowers at 60 cm (2 ft) or more with waxy white blooms. Needs full sun. *G. princeps* is smaller with jade green flowers.

Gladiolus

Plenty of popular hybrids, few of which are really hardy, and none of which likes wind. However, the rose-purple species *Gladiolus byzantinus* behaves like a weed. The late flowering *G. papilio* is surprisingly tough and has curious, pinkish-grey flowers.

Lilium

Most lilies need sheltered positions and can be difficult to establish in limy soil. But there is a strong minority of tough species which seem not to mind wind, provided their roots do not dry out. With support, *Lilium henryi* is a strong bulb, flowering with tangerine blooms at 1.8 m (6 ft) – excellent for planting between shrubs. The tiger lily, *L. tigrinum*, has vivid orange flowers with black spots and loves the sun. Pure white *L. candidum* (madonna lily), in cultivation since before the Dark Ages, has fragrant blooms in mid-summer.

AUTUMN

Colchicum

Often wrongly called autumn crocuses because their blooms resemble crocus. The leafless flowers, sometimes called 'naked ladies' or 'naked boys', appear in early autumn but are followed in spring by untidy shocks of leaves reaching 60 cm (2 ft), so careful siting is necessary. *C. speciosum* is the showiest species with lilac blooms. There is also a white form, *C. speciosum* 'Album', and a double, 'Water Lily'.

Crocus

Several good autumn flowering species naturalize in grass. Most vigorous is *C. speciosus* whose purple-blue flowers reach 10 cm (4 in) in mid-autumn. The spring foliage is far less obtrusive than with colchicums.

Cyclamen

Of the species that flower in autumn, *C. hederifolium* is the easiest, toughest and, without doubt, the most beautiful to grow. The first flowers appear before the leaves, but beautifully marbled foliage soon follows. One of the finest plants for the garden growing anywhere except in a bog.

There are many species and varieties of snowdrop. In small gardens, selecting an improved form like these Galanthus nivalis 'S. Arnott' pays dividends.

LITTLE PLANTS

Look at any famous botanical gardens and the chances are you will be astonished at the diversity of the planting. Every piece of ground is covered with living plant material of some sort, from great sprawling trees to tiny mossy saxifrages. In your own garden you should aim for something similar. Having planted the main areas, the next objective is to fill in the cracks and corners. For these you'll need small plants – often called alpines. These are useful for more than mere rock gardens. In this chapter we want to look at plants that form ground-hugging mats, plants that enjoy living underfoot, plants that will defy the windiest corner – anything that will enhance an otherwise dull stretch of ground.

Apart from their function as occupants of difficult spots, these small plants can have great beauty in their own right and are often the making of a fine garden. Some produce strong colour in certain seasons, others soften the hardness of newly constructed wall bases, steps or gateways. Paving always looks nicer with plants growing in between the stones – especially if the 'stones' are newly made concrete slabs which need mellowing to take away that awful artificial look. Border fronts always benefit from low plants and in certain situations it is often possible to furnish lawn edges with narrow borders holding collections of low growers, particularly where the lawn runs up to a wide pathway or a vehicle drive. In my own garden I allow plants to spill over from borders onto paths, seeding themselves as they like until sometimes it is difficult to see where to walk. This would be too untidy for some tastes but, on the other hand, severe and immaculate lines tend to look artificial and forbidding.

ROCK GARDENING

Rock gardening can be especially rewarding in exposed places because it is possible to construct shelter for low-growing plants by building up rockwork. Many true alpines come from habitats which are far from friendly and take kindly to bleak conditions. The golden rule with rockwork is to seek out the largest stones you can lay your hands on and to set these out to look as natural as possible. Keep any striations (patterns) in the rock running the same way and try to create little crevices between the rocks rather than merely piling up soil and then putting the stones into it like currants in a bun. There is no room here to describe rock construction in any detail but the finest way to learn, apart from reading about it, is to go out and see what others have done before you. Imitate what appeals to you but make a point of avoiding the mistakes that other people have made.

Since they are likely to serve different functions, the plants catalogued in this chapter are divided into four different groups:

COLOURFUL ALPINES

If you do build a rock garden, here are some easy alpines which will not sulk in exposed conditions. Most of them grow just as well in the front of the border or in any crevice that might occur in your garden so they will be of interest even if you've no intention of building a separate rockery. Mostly the alpines tend to flower in spring or early summer, but I've tried to include a range that will provide interest at other times of the year as well.

NOTE: All these plants enjoy sun, grow to no more than 15 cm (6 in) and are suitable for any soil type unless the text states otherwise.

Achillea
Has yellow or white flowers, and often has good foliage forming tidy mats. *A. argentea* has silver foliage and white flowers. Good yellows include *A. aurea* and *A. tomentosa*.

Alyssum
Alyssum saxatile is the toughest plant and produces glaring yellow flowers in profusion in the late spring. Try also the more attractive lemon-flowered *A. s.* 'Citrinum'.

Androsace
Lovely primula relatives which form mounds of pink or white flowers in the late spring. *A. primuloides* forms are among the easiest with pink flowers held above green foliage but *A. lanuginosa* does equally well and has silvery leaves with paler flowers.

Anthyllis
Members of the pea family. One species, *A. montana*, is easy to grow in exposed gar-

dens. The ruby flowers appear in the summer.

Aquilegia

Columbines – a large genus with some rugged species for rock gardens. *A. canadensis,* 45 cm (18 in), has red and/or yellow, spurred flowers. *A. flabellata* is blue or white and *A. discolor* is a compact gem with two-tone blue and white flowers.

Arabis

Rock cresses, a dull genus, but certain species are indestructible and are beautiful to look at. *A. albida* is well known with pink, mauve or white forms. There is a good double form. *A. ferdinandi-coburgii* has variegated foliage which makes a carpet of green and cream rosettes.

Aubrieta

For one-upmanship among plant snobs, be sure to get it spelt right and never pronounce it 'aubreesha'. Ubiquitous, but charming, rock or wall plants flowering in the spring and growing in the poorest of soils. There are smart red, pink, variegated and double forms but the common species, *A. deltoides,* is usually purplish-blue and none the worse for that.

Campanula

A vast range of bell flowers, mostly in cool colours, with *C. carpatica* having the largest flowers but *C. cochlearifolia* makes the neatest mats. *C. cochlearifolia* 'Elizabeth Oliver' has fascinating double flowers and spreads well, blooming for the second half of summer. *C. portenschlagiana,* despite its horrendous name, is grown all over Europe and spreads easily.

Cotyledon simplicifolia

Fleshy foliage above which droop 8 cm (3 in) catkin-like yellow flowers in spring. Enjoys cool conditions in semi-shade.

Dianthus

Pinks are covered on page 80 but alpine species are too useful not to mention here. Small, scented hybrid pinks include 'Pikes Pink', 'Little Jock' (pale pink) and 'Fanal' (deep red). The showiest species is *D. deltoides* which has several garden forms of which 'Flashing Light' (deep wine pink) is probably the best to buy.

Erodium

Most erodiums are too fussy to bother with in cold gardens but *E. chrysanthum* is not only fully hardy but also one of the finest 'all weather' alpines in cultivation. The silver, ferny foliage is semi-evergreen and the flowers, produced all summer in waves, are pale yellow.

Geranium

Alpine cranesbills often have brilliant pink or cerise flowers. *G. cinereum* cultivars are especially bright, usually with dark eyes. *G. cinereum* 'Ballerina' has deep cerise veining on a pale pink background. *G. farreri*, hardier than it looks, produces delicate shell pink flowers with chocolate stamens.

Hacquetia epipactis

A low growing member of the parsley family with golden flowers in green ruffs in late winter. Needs shade and moisture to survive.

Helianthemum

Small rock roses which flood the ground with colour in mid-summer. Many named varieties in cream, yellow, pink, orange and combination colours. Cut hard back after flowering to keep them young. Try the double red 'Mrs Earle' and the large-flowered 'Wisley Primrose'.

Hepatica

Shade loving, late winter flowering anemone relatives. *H. nobilis* is the easiest to grow with pure blue flowers. There are white and pink forms, many less easy to cultivate and all less attractive than the wild species.

Lithospermum

Several species and the first rate garden hybrid 'Heavenly Blue' need lime-free soil to grow well, but *Lithospermum oleifolium*, a silver-leaved subshrub with enchanting mid-blue flowers which come out in early summer, seems happy anywhere free-draining.

Penstemon

Most species are too delicate for cold gardens but *P. pinifolius* grows small, wiry stems of orange-scarlet flowers. There is a new yellow form called 'Mersea Yellow'. Although the shrubby, blue flowered *P. scouleri*, up to 45 cm (18 in), is often killed to ground level, it usually regenerates from the roots.

Phlox

The creeping North American phloxes, some of which are happiest in lime-free soil, make charming carpets. *Phlox douglasii* cultivars come in soft, pastel shades of powder-blue, mauve or white. *P. subulata* also has some brighter varieties like the shocking pink 'Crackerjack'.

Primula

A vast and variable genus with species suited to almost every situation. The European, leathery-leaved species are best suited to cold, dry conditions. *P. pubescens* and *P. marginata* have some good early spring forms including *P. marginata* 'Clear's Variety' whose leaves are coated with yellowish meal and whose flowers are pale-lilac-mauve, and *P. pubescens* 'Boothman's Ruby' which behaves like a tiny auricula with reddish-purple flowers. The alpine auriculas are easier to grow but coarser.

Ranunculus

Several first-rate garden plants though some are invasive. *R. ficaria* is a shade-tolerant weed with pretty cultivars including a showy double, 'Flore-pleno', and a pale form, 'Lemon Queen', as well as the bronze-leaved 'Brazen Hussy'. *R. gouanii* is a handsome buttercup with bold, emerald foliage and big golden blooms on short stems resembling the globe-flower (*Trollius*).

Silene

Many excellent species but one, *Silene schafta,* is doubly useful because of its mass of rich pink flowers in late summer.

Veronica

Another valuable genus. *V. rupestris* and its cultivars provide a range of colour shades in the late spring. There is a pink form, 'Mrs Holt', a white, inevitably 'Alba', and several good blues including 'Royal Blue' and the paler 'Blue Sheen'. *V. cinerea* has the added advantage of pretty, silver foliage as well as speedwell blue flowers. Cutting hard back in late winter helps to keep them compact.

Viola

There are several outstanding violets. The scented *V. odorata* and its cultivars need shade and are best grown under shrubs where they can spread without becoming a nuisance. American species such as *V. cucullata* may be scentless but make up for that by having big flowers in midspring. *V. cornuta* and its garden forms are rewarding as they flower for so long. Cut them hard back several times a season to keep them young.

CARPET PLANTS FOR CRACKS AND CORNERS

Though low growing, the following selection of plants should not be placed in rock gardens or in small borders where they will smother their neighbours. However, where it is difficult to get anything else to survive, or where a good, thick ground cover is needed to keep weeds at bay and to improve the appearance of an otherwise drab corner, these plants will work well.

Acaena

The New Zealand burrs. Rapidly spreading mats of foliage, rooting as they go. Most are windproof but some die right back to the stems in winter. *A. adscendens* has silver-grey, toothed leaves and reddish burrs. The *Acaena microphylla* hybrid 'Copper Carpet' has bronze foliage, *A. caesii-glauca* has blue-green leaves and *A. caerulea* is much larger in stem and leaf with brilliant, glaucous foliage and reddish stems. Sadly, it is less frost hardy than its other relatives but has survived temperatures down to -8°C with me. Propagate from pieces torn from the plants and replanted, or from seed.

Ajuga

Bugles. They enjoy moist soil in partial shade where they will throw rooting stolons until a carpet has formed. *Ajuga reptans* is invasive, but several garden forms have good leaves. 'Burgundy Glow' is purple, cream and green with blue flowers. *A. reptans* 'Purpurea' has a good dark leaf which sets off the blue flower spikes. *Ajuga pyramidalis* has larger leaves and more showy, intense blue flowers but must have moist, cool soil to grow well.

Geranium

More cranesbills. *G. dalmaticum* forms a thick cover, especially in free-draining soil. The flowers are clear pink and autumn foliage colour is good. A new hybrid raised at Cambridge University by crossing this species with *G. macrorrhizum (G. × cantabrigiense)*, promises to be an outstanding ground-cover plant – midway in size between its parents, with plummy-pink flowers and aromatic foliage which colours well in autumn. A single cutting grew to a mat more than 1 m (3¼ ft) across in one season on my soil.

Lysimachia nummularia

Creeping jenny, a vigorous, but charming, ground runner with golden flowers produced all summer. Likes moisture but also happy in full sun. There is also a gold-leaved form.

Scutellaria scordifolia

There are several good skullcaps but *S. scordifolia*, though it dies away to nothing in winter, forms a thick mat of nettle-like leaves with deep blue, well-shaped flowers for a long time in summer.

Sedum

The humble ones – *S. acre, S. telephium fabaria, S. album* and *S. spathulifolium* are especially good because they grow, where nothing else will, in the driest crevices. *S. spurium* has some pretty garden forms, as does *S. telephium*.

PLANTS FOR PAVING

Here are some plants which are especially good for establishing between paving slabs.

Planting living plants between narrow cracks is not easy. You may need to slice them in half and pare down the rootstock with an old knife to get it small enough to slot in. This may seem rather drastic but, as long as you plant early enough in the spring to allow them to develop a root system before the dry weather comes, you'll be surprised at how quickly they get established and start seeding.

Alchemilla
Ladies' mantle. Three species are excellent in paving. *A. conjuncta* and *A. alpina* are almost identical with silver-lined foliage and little green, musk-scented flowers. *A. pumila* 'Faroensis' is like a compact version with rounded leaves. They all seed freely.

Armeria maritima
Common thrift, whose natural habitat is clifftop turf, will establish itself in paving. The pink of the flowers looks particularly good with grey stone.

Draba
Most of them are drab but *D. aizoides* has tight rosettes and little yellow flowers in late winter.

Dryas octopetala
A relic from the ice age, which is happy in the bleakest conditions and flowers well even if the roots are restricted between paving. Has oak-like, evergreen leaves and cream rose-shaped flowers in early summer.

Erigeron mucronatus
Unlike other members of this genus, *E. mucronatus* has thin, wiry stems and an endless succession of pink and white daisy flowers. It seeds very freely but parent plants are often killed off by a hard winter.

Erinus
A 'state of the art' paving plant which survives foot pressure, wind and heat or cold. It is short lived, but seeds freely. There are three colour forms – pink, white or red.

Iris
A surprising entry, but dwarf irises flower so well if their roots are crammed between paving stones. Getting them planted is well nigh impossible but if there is a little corner or a hole, give them a try, pushing the roots down but leaving the rhizomes on top.

Saxifraga

Another enormous and varied genus. The more commonplace species like *Saxifraga ×
urbium* (London pride) are very happy in paving. Look out for 'Elliot's Form', which is compact, and for variegated London pride which has a bonus of bright winter foliage – red, cream and green.

Sedum

These are paving plants *par excellence* being easy to establish and quick to recover from damage by passing feet, kids' bikes, dogs, etc. See 'carpeters' page 105.

Sempervivum

Houseleeks which form well-shaped rosettes of fleshy leaves. There are many species and varieties: choose the most common as these are likely to be the toughest.

Sisyrinchium

Most are unsuitable for paving but *S. bermudianum* (blue) and its odd brown-flowered sport 'Quaint and Queer' or 'Biscutellum' grow well in stone and one can keep them under control that way.

Most sisyrinchiums seed a little too freely.

Thymus

The finest of all paving plants because they run along the cracks, rooting as they go. Walking on thyme, on a hot terrace, brings out the aromatic smell. The flower colours, particularly of the *Thymus serpyllum* cultivars, are rich and pleasing. For flowers, look for *T. serpyllum* 'Pink Chintz' which is clean, pale pink, 'Russettings' (purple) and 'Albus'. For pretty foliage, try 'Anderson's Gold' or 'Doone Valley' (yellow, red and green leaves, lilac flowers). Variegated lemon thyme, especially the clone called 'Nyewoods', is good and *T. caespititius* has tiny leaves with pretty lavender flowers.

Viola

Dog violets – *Viola. riviniana* and *V. labradorica* will seed freely in paving and flower well in the shade. Look for the pink form which seems to be even more prolific than the white. Small yellow *V. biflora* should grow well in paving in the shade.

DWARF SHRUBS

Before leaving this chapter, we should spare a thought for the dwarf shrubs. Where we are adding to our gardens, rather than planning the basic planting, we need to add some charm and interest. In winter, a tiny, twiggy willow, graced with silver catkins, or a daphne in full flower among its dormant neighbours, will give you that extra boost of enjoyment which all good gardens should provide.

Because some gardens are so small, it often pays to miniaturise mixed borders. Dwarf shrubs, in these instances, provide the necessary backbone to the planting without going out of proportion. Sinks and containers, where gardening is always miniaturised, can be boring during the winter. A dwarf holly or tiny conifer will give you that interest until the next growing season begins.

Artemisia

Though not really dwarf and only just shrubs, one or two species, cut hard back in late summer, have useful silver foliage in winter. *Artemisia* 'Powys Castle' is especially hardy with silver filigree leaves. *A. schmidtiana* 'Nana' has leaves like silver feathers but needs regular cutting back to keep it neat, and it dies if it gets too damp in winter.

Chamaecyparis lawsoniana 'Minima Glauca'

A tiny, rounded, slow-growing conifer.

Cheiranthus

These are not really shrubs either but do form bushy plants with rigid stems. In exposed gardens they will not live long but are easy to propagate from cuttings taken in late summer and overwintered in a frame. *Cheiranthus linifolius* 'Bowles Mauve' has the best foliage and constant purple flowers. *C.* 'Harpur Crewe' is double yellow, with double the petals, double the scent.

Daphne

Two species exist for exposed gardens. *D. cneorum* stays low and is crowned with rich pink flowers that smell exquisite. Mulch each summer with peaty compost to encourage extra growth from the crown. *D. collina* is evergreen with pink flowers in the spring.

Erica

Plus calluna and daboecia – the heathers. Don't overdo heathers but they are so valuable for evergreen cover and necessary winter colour. Most need acid soil but for limy gardens, late summer flowering *Erica terminalis* is the happiest.

Genista

Also, cytisus. Dwarf brooms, mostly yellow. *Genista sagittalis* creeps with flattened stems and flowers that look like the feathering on arrows. *Genista lydia* has curving green stems and a dazzling display of golden blossom in early summer. *G. tinctoria* (dyer's greenweed) has a good double form for gardens, and the little creeping *Cytisus de-*

cumbens is a contour hugger which will cascade over the side of a container.

Hebe

Already mentioned on page 65 but good dwarf varieties include 'Carl Teschner' which has blue flowers, *H. pinguifolia* 'Pagei' which has pretty grey leaves and 'Boughton Dome' which looks like a tiny, humped conifer. The smaller the leaves, they say, the hardier the hebe.

Ilex

Several dwarf hollies make good container shrubs. *Ilex crenata* has tiny leaves and grows slowly. *I.* × *hascombensis* is a neat grower with deep, glossy leaves. They're all shade tolerant.

Juniperus communis 'Compressa'

A dwarf conifer with tight, erect branches which grows so slowly it stays small for decades. Perfect for sink or trough growing.

Picea abies 'Nidiformis'

A tiny, stunted christmas tree which hardly grows but stays green in colour. *P. abies* 'Gre-goryana' is also small and stunted, forming a spiky green blob the size of a football in a dozen years.

Potentilla

Popular dwarf shrubs which can be hacked into submission if they do exceed 75 cm (2½ ft) which they seldom do. They flower for a long season from early summer onwards and come in various shades of yellow – 'Elizabeth', white – 'Abbotswood' and orange – 'Tangerine'.

Rhododendron

For acid soils, there are many small, slow-growing species. Showy dwarf hybrids include the *R. yakushimanum* group. 'Bluebird' is even lower with small leaves and violet-blue flowers.

Salix

Mentioned a lot already in the text, this genus has such outstanding dwarf species that its name was bound to appear again. Try *S.* × *boydii* for twigginess or *S. arbuscula* for a trailing mass of stems. *S. subopposita* has leaves opposite, meaning twice the number of catkins per stem.

FOOD FROM EXPOSED PLACES

The basic principles for growing food are exactly the same as for ornamental plants. The objective is to ensure healthy, happy specimens by providing a good growing environment. Thherefore all the remarks in previous chapters about creating shelter will also apply to the kitchen garden.

PREPARING THE GROUND

Assuming the measures discussed in part one have been taken, we can now turn our attention to the specific needs of growing vegetables.

Soil

Nothing can grow in the spring until the ground has warmed up sufficiently. Windy conditions will slow down the rate at which soil temperatures rise. Saturation with water is another factor – the wetter the ground the colder it is. Heavy clay is the slowest to come to life as it clings to its water for so much longer.

The first solution, therefore, is to keep the weather away from the ground. Traditionally, this was done by placing glass cloches over bare ground. They acted as mini-greenhouses, warming the soil and allowing any sur-

Woodland floor, meadow or rock garden all make equally suitable homes for the snakeshead fritillary Fritillaria meleagris.

plus moisture to evaporate. Later, vegetable seeds were put under the cloches and, when these germinated, the glass gave the young plants a good start in life and protection from frost. This system is still widely used but is so much easier today with the availability of plastic mulches, sheeting, cloches and frames.

With sheeting, whole stretches of soil can be dried and warmed. Later, plants can be inserted through holes punched in the film at intervals, so that their roots are warmed and protected for the first part of their lives. Take care though, plastic sheeting is ugly, gets caught in the wind, does not rot, and will need to be tactfully positioned. Even the field frames, though they are constructed with strong metal tubing, act as sails and can soon become airborne unless securely anchored down.

Position
Although different flowering plants can be found which are suitable for sun or shade, all vegetables and most fruits

Autumn bulbs such as these Colchicum autumnale *naturalize well in grass but are equally at home in the mixed border. Remember though, they have large, ugly leaves in spring.*

must have full sun. If you are constructing rigid windbreaks this must be borne in mind. If you plant in rows, these should stretch north-south with a shelter hedge or fence to the north. In bleak spots, carefully positioned screens on either side will help to keep wind off.

In gardens where the kitchen garden is being incorporated into the design because it is difficult to conceal, consider growing in blocks or patterns so that the food looks pretty as well as being good to eat. Trimming such kitchen gardens with cordon apples, with herbs and with occasional cutting flowers can give a charming effect and will be useful in a culinary sense too.

The choice
Delicious though they are, fresh vegetables from your garden will usually have cost you more than they would at the greengrocer. It is therefore not worth struggling with crops that dislike your soil conditions and it is profitless to grow vegetables which are not better fresh than stored. Maincrop potatoes come into this cateogory, as do carrots, swedes, turnips, parsnips and big solid winter cabbage. On the other hand, salad materials, broccoli, peas and beans, spinach and tomatoes are all far nicer fresh so these are the types of plant on which to concentrate.

The actual growing of all the usual vegetables is simplicity itself. First, get your soil prepared by digging in manure in the autumn, then working it down in spring until friable. Also apply an organic based or compound fertilizer, following the manufacturer's instructions, unless the soil is already heavily fertilized with manure.

Follow the instructions regarding sowing dates and depths on the packets, making sure you have a good, crumbly moist seedbed. Later, some plants will need thinning out or transplanting but it is always better to sow thinly rather than too densely. Mark rows carefully and begin hoeing out the weeds as soon as the vegetable seedlings have emerged.

Continuity
If you want heavy, year-round production you will need to plan ahead carefully. Detailed vegetable skills are beyond the scope of this book but here is a table suggesting the kind of rotation and continuity you should be able to achieve.

Special precautions
Where wind is particularly

troublesome, taller brassicas like Brussels sprouts, which will still be in the ground in midwinter, should be supported by tying the plants to canes or stakes. On sandy soils, very young seedlings can be protected from windblow by pushing pea sticks or twigs into the ground at angles or, by sowing in unfilled trenches. Cordon fruits help here, especially where dwarf varieties are used, so that they do not grow up to throw too much shade onto the garden.

A greenhouse
However sheltered the garden may be, if it freezes in winter, a greenhouse is useful. In a cold, exposed area, a greenhouse will transform your life. Apart from the obvious advantages of providing facilities for raising your own seedlings and cuttings more easily and providing winter protection for tender plants, a greenhouse also gives you a month or two of extra growing season.

With hardy vegetables like Brussels sprouts and leeks, sowing in late winter under glass makes for better plants. Sowing in trays, pricking out into small pots and then planting these later may sound complicated but it is actually much easier than raising the same plants in seed beds outside.

When it comes to tender crops like French beans, courgettes, tomatoes, sweetcorn or peppers, a greenhouse is almost essential, not necessarily to grow them in, but to get the young plants off to an early start . Seed is sown in late winter under glass to provide established plants for setting out as soon as the frost season has passed.

The disadvantage to all this is the cost of heating. There are various ways of keeping this to a minimum:

1 Make sure the structure is heat-efficient. Double glazing is expensive but may pay for itself within a few years. There are various insulating sheets available which are easy to attach to the sides and roof. Lean-to greenhouses, especially if they are leaning to a thick, south-facing wall, tend to retain their heat longer. Draught-free ventilation is important and you must be able to open all windows and even the door during bright winter days.

2 Select the cheapest heat source. Portable bottled gas heaters are inexpensive to run, can be fitted with thermostats and have the added bonus of supplying extra carbon dioxide, essential to

plants, as a product of combustion. Other methods of heating include paraffin, electricity, wood, coal or other solid fuels and your choice will depend on what is most convenient and economic in your area.

3 Opt for the lowest minimum temperatures. For raising food, a small electric propagator which enables seed to germinate in soils at around 20°C (68°F) will allow you to save on the space heating in the greenhouse. Merely keeping the remainder frost free [say a minimum 2°C (35°F)] will suffice for all vegetables and most flower seedlings. In the spring the greenhouse can grow tomatoes, aubergines, peppers and cucumbers, for example, or, chrysanthemums for cutting in autumn. The propagator will be used for striking cuttings during the summer too and will give you better results with some autumn sown flower seeds as well.

FRUIT

Besides vegetables and salad materials, any garden, however bleak and exposed, should be able to produce at least some fruit. The colder the area, the more limited the choice, but there are plenty of apples, plums and pears that will yield reasonably well even in sub-arctic conditions.

Soft fruit
Raspberries and strawberries
Good soil is essential to achieve good results. Work in plenty of humus and keep it fertile by dressing with fertilizer every year. Virus is the eternal bugbear with raspberries and strawberries. To avoid it, don't grow them in one spot for too long, always buy from a reputable source and never accept plants from a well-meaning friend! Strawberries can be grown through a plastic sheet and will fruit early under cloches. They must have full sun but raspberries tolerate partial shade. Raspberry canes must be cut to the ground after fruiting and new growths limited to about six canes per stool. They are shallow-rooted and will benefit from a thick mulch in summer to reduce any soil moisture loss.

Black currants and gooseberries
Though self-fertile, gooseberry and black currant bushes flower early in spring and the blossom can sometimes be wiped out by late frost. Protection with a plastic sheet when frost is forecast will help but see page 55 on

Frost Pockets. Fertile soil is important and you'll need to watch for mildew and gooseberry sawfly in the gooseberries and big-bud in the black currants. Wood that has just fruited should always be cut hard back to promote new growth.

Top fruit
Apples

The apple is such a beautiful tree with its spring blossom, pleasant bark and colourful fruits, that it would be worth growing even if they were inedible. Select a self-pollinating variety but all apples fruit better in the presence of a pollinator – either another, matched variety or one of the pollen-bearing ornamental crabs. A free-standing apple tree needs pruning to ensure good yield and shapely growth. Prevent branches from crossing over and remove young shoots to the bottom three buds to promote fruiting spurs.

Alternatively, apples and pears can be grown as cordons, linked to horizontal wires suspended between posts, or as espaliers.

As with soft fruit, late frost can wreak havoc with the blossoms but this is more likely in a frost pocket than in a hilltop garden. Wind can cause problems by damaging young foliage and blowing off the ripening fruit. Growing dwarf or cordon trees helps to circumvent this destruction but it still pays to make sure your wind-proofing around the boundaries is adequate.

Plums

Plums and damsons are often more capable of coping with wind than are apples and pears. They can even be used as windbreak trees to protect apples and pears within. Though susceptible to late frosts, most are self fertile and do not need pollinators. Old favourites like 'Czar' and 'Victoria' are still popular. Pruning must not be done during winter when silver-leaf fungus could enter through unhealed wounds.

WALLS

When contemplating food production, don't forget that your walls and fences could make perfect sites for growing fruit. Even if your garden is too exposed for them to yield well when free standing, peaches, nectarines, apples, pears, some cherries and even figs could all thrive trained on a west or south wall, looking attractive and providing food.

Soft fruit will also grow against a wall, not only trailing plants like blackberries,

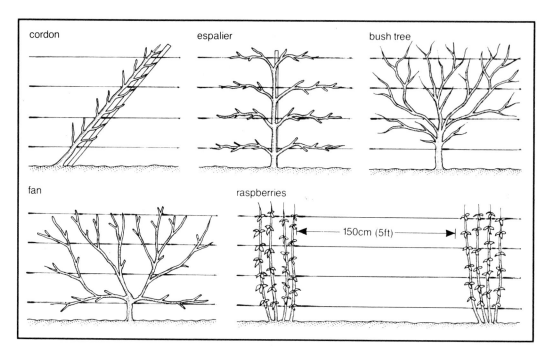

Fig. 9. Different methods of training wall plants onto walls or fences. Herbaceous climbers can be allowed to scramble amongst these once they have become established.

and tayberries but also gooseberries and redcurrants. The wall both protects the fruit and hastens ripening and, in excessively cold areas, may be the only way you can be assured of a heavy crop.

Cherries seldom fruit well in cold districts but may well perform on a wall provided they are netted from the birds. In marginal areas, free-standing cherries can yield better crops if large sheets of polythene are thrown over them and kept in place by bird netting.

Food for the non kitchen gardener

Finally, even if you don't have the room or inclination for a full-blown vegetable garden, try growing the border plant *Crambe maritima,* for example, which has lovely foliage but is also suitable for spring blanching and makes succulent eating. Ruby chard, a gorgeous red-stemmed leaf vegetable makes good eating and one of my mixed borders even boasts a statuesque patch of rhubarb. There are ornamental cabbages and kales; tomatoes and red peppers look pretty in summer and globe artichokes, if you have room, make impressive border plants.

There are few ugly herbs and therefore no excuse at all

SOWING	HARVESTING/PLANTING
January – March (midwinter – early spring)	
Place cloches/sheeting	
Sow: carrots, lettuce, radish, onions, calabrese (under protection) Plant: chitted first early potatoes, artichokes, asparagus crowns.	Brussels sprouts, kale, winter savoy, leeks.
April – June (spring-early summer)	
Sow: sprouts, cauliflower, lettuce, peas, French beans, courgettes Plant: sprouts, cauliflowers, courgettes, tomatoes, peppers	Broad beans, spinach, radish, lettuce, first new potatoes, asparagus, spring onions
July – September (summer – early autumn)	
Sow: winter salads, lettuce, Plant: winter cabbage, kale, Brussels sprouts	Everything – peas, beans, carrots, new potatoes, calabrese, etc.
October – December (autumn – winter)	
Sow: broad beans	Sprouts and other brassicas, leeks, parsnips, Jerusalem artichokes.

for not having at least the usual kitchen essentials like sage, rosemary, parsley, tarragon, marjoram and thyme as well as a selection of mints.

Apart from mints, which are liable to become invasive nuisances, herbs will not only enjoy life in mixed borders but will add to their charm. Sage comes in a variety of foliage colours of which the purple is probably hardiest, followed closely by the gold variegated *Salvia officinalis* 'Icterina'. Planted together they contrast pleasingly and in the company of traditional 'cottage' plants they are superb. Thyme makes a delightful paving plant or will populate a very dry sunny bank, keeping company with rock roses and marjoram.

POLICING THE SYSTEM

Gardening is a dynamic art form. It changes day by day, year by year and it is in the constant change that the charm of a good garden lies. Once you have achieved the first objective – converting the garden from an exposed site into a sheltered haven for plants – you will then be able to move on to the even more satisfying occupation of fine tuning.

I have avoided the word maintenance because although there are always routine jobs like weeding, pruning and fertilizing to be done, these are fitted into a constant run of appraisal. As you work through your borders, removing sowthistles or digging out stubborn pockets of couchgrass, you will notice how some plants are doing particularly well, while others seem to have stood still. As the growth matures you'll find newly shaded areas, new sun traps, mystery spots which seem to dry out too quickly or patches that stay wet all the time and so on. There will also be surprise introductions and unwelcome ones, like nettles and docks, of course, but pleasant ones too, like foxgloves perhaps or holly seedlings. You will have made mistakes – planted trees too close together, shrubs wrongly placed, colour clashes or injudicious pruning. These seldom emerge at once but become apparent and are rectified over the years. The purpose of this final chapter is to offer a little guidance, not just on how to maintain, but on how to get the most satisfaction out of your garden over those years.

WEEDS

However clean your ground may be and regardless of how many gallons of agrochemicals you throw about, there will always be weeds. A weed is often defined as being a plant growing in the wrong place: but what is the wrong place? Hard to say, clearly – it's a question of coming to terms with what you want and where you want it. It pays to be unprejudiced about a plant's origins and to decide whether it's welcome of not, basing your decision not on what the plant is but whether it is suitable for that position in your border. My garden

Easiest and brightest of all rock plants, Aubrieta deltoides *is far too good to be despised. There are various colours and also double and variegated forms.*

contains self-introduced 'weeds' like red campion, harebells and meadow cranesbill which I tolerate. There are also primroses and foxgloves – all volunteers, which I happily encourage.

Perennial weeds
Certain weeds, however, are bad news and of those, perennials are the very worst. Couchgrass, ground elder, creeping buttercup, creeping cinquefoil, bindweed (greater and lesser) stinging nettles, willowherb and perennial deadnettles are all evil pests. Not only do they come again and again from a creeping rootstock, they seed as well. A constant war needs to be waged against them.

Any chemical treatment must attack the *system* of the plant rather than merely burning off the foliage. Glyphosate is the most effective provided it is applied during good growing conditions and provided there is no rain for six hours after application. One drop of glyphosate on the wrong plant is lethal so extreme care is essential when treating perennial weeds in established borders. A small hand sprayer is useful or a brush to paint chemical directly onto the leaves of the weed. If you do contaminate a plant, sprinkle it copiously with water to wash the glyphosate off the leaves. The chemical cannot be absorbed from the soil.

Digging can help, provided all the root is removed. In practice this is very difficult unless the ground is dug over several times but a constant attack on these weeds will reward you with a gradual diminution of numbers.

Annual weeds
The old adage 'One year's seed means ten years' weed', unlike most old sayings, is accurate. The secret of annual weed control is to prevent seeding. They cannot reproduce in any other way so you would expect eradication to be easy but the number of seeds a single annual plant can produce is phenomenal. If you spot an outbreak of groundsel, fools' parsley, sow thistles, speedwell, shepherd's purse or poppies (in the wrong place), clear them out before they flower.

One particular scourge is hairy bittercress (*Cardamine hirsuta*). It is one of the less savoury by-products of the containerised plant industry and once in your soil the seed is almost impossible to eliminate. Plants are able to germinate, flower and set seed in a few weeks so one missed plant will soon spread wildly –

so be vigilant.

Having healthy, well stocked borders will go a long way towards eliminating the worst of the annual weeds because the competition from your ground cover and other plants will tend to smother them out. Thick mulches also help but can sometimes inhibit plants which you want to multiply from self-sowing. It depends on the material and the thickness.

CHEMICALS

Many people are concerned about using chemicals in the garden. It is perfectly possible to run an excellent garden without using chemical sprays or fertilizers at all. There will be more hard work at times and disease control will not be as efficient, particularly on roses, but good gardening is still perfectly feasible. If you do use chemicals keep chemical applications in the garden to the absolute minimum necessary for control.

FEEDING

Most of the plant's body is manufactured from carbon, hydrogen and oxygen. These materials are in the atmosphere so you might say that mighty oaks appear out of

Here are some simple rules for safe use of chemicals.
1   Always read and obey the instructions on the package.
2   Don't stock-pile – store as little as you can.
3   Never transfer a chemical to a different container. Don't let labels rot off or tins rust through.
4   Never keep diluted product. Dilute enough to use and discard any remainder safely.
5   Always wash your sprayer thoroughly after use.
6   Try to spray insecticide when there are no bees about.
7   Wear rubber gloves and wash your hands thoroughly after spraying. Do not allow any chemical to touch your skin.
8   Discard old or unwanted material safely.

thin air! To carry out this miracle they need water and certain minerals, the chief ones being nitrogen, phosphorus and potassium. They also need iron, sulphur, magnesium, manganese, calcium, copper and boron in smaller quantities. Most of these minerals, in natural conditions, are available in the right quantities to suit plant life. An over-simplified picture of course, but that is basically it.

All gardens are, to some extent, artificial environments. You will be cutting dead perennials back in autumn and taking them away, along with some minerals. As well as putting this back in the form of compost, use fertilizer which is rich in the three main minerals – nitrogen, phosphorus and potassium (N, P and K). Quantities and frequency depend on what kind of soil you have, how fertile it is already and what you intend to grow. In my own garden I throw a compound containing 15% each of N, P and K – about every spring at a very approximate rate of 30g per m^2 (1oz per sq yd). Areas I deem impoverished get a little more, others might get missed altogether. I also try to mulch all the borders at least once in three years with rotted manure, compost or spent mushroom compost.

Vegetables need more food. Routinely I scatter the same 15% NPK compound at about 60g per m^2 (2oz per sq yd) evenly over the surface before sowing seed and place about 30g (1 oz) for each potato in the trench alongside the tubers. Building up fertility gradually over the years will reflect in the size of your yields. When cases of urgent need become apparent, sometimes in the form of reduced growth rate and pale green foliage, try using an extra top dressing or some proprietory liquid fertilizer.

I dislike over-fed flowering plants and suspect that the fertilizing gospel is preached rather too fervently in some quarters. Good soil conditions, adequate drainage and careful planting are every bit as important as opening the fertilizer bag.

PLANT HEALTH

The plants listed in preceding chapters are robust and should be able to resist most plant diseases. But roses are the big exception. They are susceptible to two serious fungal infections – mildew and blackspot. Without sprays, both these diseases will be endemic in your garden. Even with regular spraying, certain varieties will show signs of one or other of them every year. Because roses play such an important part in exposed gardens, you will need to come to terms with this major weakness. Organic gardeners must restrict themselves to species that are resistant – especially the rugosas – but even then, in some years there will still be disease.

Mildew does not kill, but disfigures the foliage by covering it with a white powdery bloom. Eventually, the leaves wrinkle and flowers are spoilt. Roses on warm walls and in sheltered positions are especially susceptible. Blackspot begins as dark marks on mature foliage; eventually these turn yellow and the plant begins to defoliate. Blackspot can kill susceptiable varieties within a season.

Treatment: prevention is better than cure. Spray every 14 days during the growing season with a systemic fungicide designed to attack both mildew and blackspot. These days, there are several brands available containing cocktails of chemicals to attack both fungi. More traditional blackspot cures include copper and sulphur compounds.

Apart from these rose diseases, spots, rots and wilts are bound to occur elsewhere from time to time, but as long as you look after your soil condition and fertility health should prevail. There are disastrous diseases such as fireblight which destroys members of the rose family other than roses and a horrible fungus – honey fungus – which attacks all woody plants. Phytophthora kills off tree and shrub roots. If you notice parts of shrubs or whole shrubs dying, you'll need to get some professional advice.

FELLOW HORTICULTURISTS

The joy of gardening is that there are so many like-minded souls about. Learning from others is made easy because most enthusiasts are ready and willing to share their passion with you. Joining any of the horticultural societies will help, not only to introduce you to the experts but also to meet people with similar gardens. Many societies have seed exchange systems and circulate helpful and interesting literature among their members. The Royal Horticultural Society, famous for the Chelsea Flower Show, has a vast range of facilities including gardens at Wisley and elsewhere, educational facilities, regular flower shows in London and a plant health and garden advisory service. Find out about your local societies and join them – you'll find it worthwhile.

APPENDIX

WHERE TO SEE EXPOSED GARDENS

If you are looking for inspiration from other gardens, perhaps for good planting combinations or simply to see first hand the range of plants that will do well on exposed sites, there are plenty of good gardens to visit.

In Britain we are fortunate in having many excellent gardens open to the public, including many under the National Gardens Scheme. Gardens open under this scheme have not been included here because they are generally open to the public for a limited period during the year, and the days may vary from year to year. However, the gardens listed are open for at least several months of the year, but not necessarily every day. It is well worth checking the opening times in advance if possible.

Garden visiting is a wonderful pastime anyway, so it makes sense to try to fit in a few visits to exposed gardens on your holidays and when travelling around the country. Some of the famous ones will be found in the list below, and all are well worth visiting for their general horticultural merit anyway. The list is by no means exhaustive.

Don't forget to take a notebook and pencil with you when you go garden visiting in order to jot down names of plants that appeal to you. Also make notes of any particularly attractive plant associations that you come across.

Anglesey Abbey, Lode, Cambridge, Cambridgeshire
6 miles NE of Cambridge, on the B1102. A National Trust Garden. Formal and landscaped divided gardens. Avenues of trees, hedged enclosures. Superb planting schemes.

Belton House, Grantham, Lincolnshire
3 miles NE of Grantham on the A607. National Trust Garden. Formal gardens, and orangery.

Boughton House, Geddington, Kettering, Northamptonshire
3 miles N of Kettering, off the A43 (on the Geddington to Grafton Underwood road). The Duke of Buccleuch and Queensberry. Magnificent collections of trees, lily pools, rose gardens, herbaceous border, etc.

Castle Drogo, Drewsteignton, Devon
4 miles S of A30 via Crockernwell. National Trust. A garden of medium size featuring collections of shrubs and woodland walk.

Castle Howard, York, North Yorkshire
5 miles W of Malton; situated between the roads B1257 and A64. Noted for its extensive formal and woodland gardens; large walled garden with vast collection of shrub roses.

Doddington Hall, nr Lincoln, Lincolnshire
5 miles SW of Lincoln. From Lincoln via A46 turn W onto B1190 for Doddington. Walled gardens.

Felbrigg Hall, Roughton, Norfolk
2½ miles SW of Cromer, S of A148; entrance from B1436. The National Trust. Noted for shrubs, orangery which contains camellias, and walled garden.

Kiftsgate Court, Chipping Campden, Gloucestershire
3 miles NE of Chipping Campden, 1 mile E of A46 and B4081. Noted for its collection of unusual shrubs and other plants; good collection of roses.

Knightshayes Court, Bolham, Tiverton, Devon
2 miles N of Tiverton; turn E off the A396 at Bolham. The national Trust. Rare and unusual plants; roses, perennials, rhododendrons, bulbs; several small gardens, woodland gardens.

Polesden Lacey, nr Dorking, Surrey
3 miles NW of Dorking; turn S off the A246 at Great Bookham. The National Trust. Enclosed gardens, rose garden, mixed borders, shrubs, trees, rock and shrub banks.

Rockingham Castle, Rockingham, Northamptonshire
3 miles NW of Corby on the A6003. Four distinct gardens, including a wild garden and rose garden. Park with specimen trees.

IBLIOGRAPHY

BONAR, Ann *Garden Plant Survival Manual, The* Ward Lock, 1988.
BROWNE, Janet *Ground Cover Plants* Ward Lock, 1988.
Hillier's Manual of Trees and Shrubs David and Charles, 1981.
NORTH, Felicity *Gardening in a Cold Climate* Collingridge, 1967.
RICE, Graham *Plants for Problem Places* Christopher Helmt Timber Press, 1988.
SMITH, Geoffrey *Easy Plants for Difficult Places* Hamlyn, 1984.
TOOGOOD, Alan *Border Plants* Ward Lock, 1987.
TOOGOOD, Alan *Hedges and Boundaries* Salamander, 1986.
TOOGOOD, Alan *Secret Gardens* Ward Lock, 1987.
WILLIAMS, Hugh *Hamlyn Guide to Plant Selection, The* Hamlyn, 1988.

ACKNOWLEDGMENTS

The publishers are grateful to the following for kindly granting permission for their photographs to be included in this book: Pat Brindley (p75); Photos Horticultural (pp 2/3, 11, 14, 19, 34, 39, 43, 50, 54, 58, 67, 78, 95, 98, 110) and Harry Smith Collection (pp 7, 23, 42, 47, 59, 71, 74, 86, 87, 91, 94, 111, 119).

All line drawings by John Woodcock.

INDEX